S0-DRZ-082

Junior Broadway

Junior Broadway

How to Produce Musicals with Children 9 to 13

SECOND EDITION

by Beverly B. Ross *and*
Jean P. Durgin

A15015 277807

MT
955
.R67
1998
West

McFarland & Company, Inc, Publishers
Jefferson, North Carolina and London

All photos (except pages 77 and 114) by Richard J. Durgin.

Front cover photo: Mrs. Anna and the King waltz to "Shall We Dance?" in *The King and I.*

Frontispiece: A tender moment for Harold Hill and Marian the Librarian in *The Music Man.*

This book is dedicated to
The Backstage Joy Boys
and to all the children who have
ever been a part of one of our shows

British Library Cataloguing-in-Publication data are available

Library of Congress Cataloguing-in-Publication Data

Ross, Beverly B., 1931–
    Junior Broadway : how to produce musicals with children 9
to 13 / by Beverly B. Ross and Jean P. Durgin. — 2nd ed.
        p.   cm.
    ISBN 0-7864-0341-1 (sewn softcover : 50# alkaline paper) ∞
    1. Musicals—Stage guides.   2. Amateur theater—Production
and direction.   3. Children's plays—Presentation, etc.
I. Durgin, Jean P., 1941–   . II. Title.
MT955.R67   1998
792.6'0232—dc21   98-47309
                                                            CIP
                                                            MN

©1998 Beverly B. Ross and Jean P. Durgin. All rights reserved

No part of this book, specifically including the table of contents
and index, may be reproduced or transmitted in any form or by
any means, electronic or mechanical, including photocopying or
recording, or by any information storage and retrieval system,
without permission in writing from the publisher.

Manufactured in the United States of America

McFarland & Company, Inc., Publishers
  Box 611, Jefferson, North Carolina 28640

Contents

Preface to the Second Edition

We are very grateful to all our readers and enthusiastic fans who have used the ideas and techniques set forth in our original edition of this book. When it was written we had produced plays with children for five years. The second edition includes everything we have learned in 11 more years of experience in producing musicals with those wonderful children.

You may notice that, although *Junior Broadway* has two authors, the chapters are written from the viewpoint of one person. This was a comfortable format for us, and we hope it will prove comfortable for the reader as well. Because one of us was the producer-director of the shows and the other handled the artwork and technical details, our work did not overlap. Each of us had our own areas of expertise, and we wrote accordingly.

The chapters are organized in a way that will lead you through the process of producing a Broadway-type musical play with children. From choosing the play to the final bows, the book takes you through each step along the way.

We hope you will find lots of new ideas that you can use in this edition. We wish you lots of luck and bushels of fun!

1

A Broadway Musical: Why, Who and How?

CEDAR PARK ELEMENTARY SCHOOL PRESENTS *The Music Man*! Your eyes focus on the banner headline in the local newspaper. "Oops! Must be a misprint." Then, as you read the first paragraph, you learn that indeed young school children are actually going to try to perform a Broadway show! How absurd! Yet, as an elementary-school teacher yourself, you cannot help but be interested. As you continue through the article, your interest heightens. Then you note that the show will be presented that Friday evening in a junior high school near your home. "This I have to see!" You think you know what to expect, but just in case you are wrong, you decide to attend.

On Friday night, as you drive up to the school, you behold a mob scene. Where will you park? The front lot is full. For a kids' show? Maybe you have really stumbled onto something!

Seated about two-thirds of the way back from the stage in the closest seat you could find, you glance at your program. You note that all of the children in the cast are fifth graders. The list of adult helpers covers the full-page insert of the program. Someone has gone to much effort at any rate. The lights dim, the curtain opens, and you gaze toward the stage.

An hour and a half later as the finale ends, you sit in your chair, stunned! All around you people are clapping and cheering. The stage is full of beaming children costumed in black pants, red taffeta tunics and matching hats trimmed with gold braid. Waves of applause roll over them! The children repeat the finale as an encore, but the audience does not quiet down. They continue clapping, now in time to the music. They rise as one to give these wondrous children the tribute

3

Finale of *The Music Man.*

of a standing ovation. As the curtain closes, the roof seems to lift from the building with the deafening roar from the audience!

There are goose bumps on your arms and tears in your eyes. How is it possible, this performance that you have just seen? You have clearly understood the nuance of every word of the play and every song. Fifth graders! Ten-year-old children!

> ➤ How did they do it?
> ➤ Who taught them such professionalism?
> ➤ Where did their teacher find the time?
> ➤ Was that two-part harmony I heard?
> ➤ How many weeks did they rehearse?
> ➤ How much did the costumes cost?
> ➤ How many adults helped?
> ➤ Did the children really paint that marvelous scenery themselves?

Perhaps the first question should be, *Why* should a fifth grade class put on a Broadway musical? What does it offer to the teacher and to her students that makes such an undertaking worthwhile? Drama training? Voice training? A teacher has enough to keep her busy. She must give her students a proper background in math, reading, spelling and many other subjects in order to produce adults capable of coping with this modern world. Drama and singing are far down the list of essentials that an average person must learn, particularly at the elementary-school level. Why, then, should she do it?

A good teacher knows that the most important thing she can give her students is a sense of self-worth and the confidence to attempt new things. Children must learn to work in a group, and no social studies or science projects can teach teamwork as can a play. Students and teacher alike must learn to organize their time efficiently when they have to balance homework with after-school rehearsals, and still allow time for piano lessons, sports, scouting and all the other activities in which they are involved. How about the students who get into mischief when they have too much time on their hands? Solution: a play will fill that extra time.

A teacher does not undertake a project that steals her precious after-school hours without some benefit to herself. That benefit for me is *joy*. Such a simple three-letter word, but it says it all. To see ten-year-old children eagerly volunteer to stay after school for a minimum of 45 minutes a day, five days a week, for three months is an achievement in itself. To see the shy child, desperately seeking the approval of classmates yet afraid he or she will not gain it, finally act, sing or dance on a stage in front of several hundred people is remarkable. The self-confidence young children gain in a project of this kind stays with them for the rest of their lives.

The popular, self-confident child is not the main winner in a play. He gains, as do all the children. Yet that child will survive in this world with a high degree of success. It is the others, those who have never felt they were the masters of their fate, who benefit most. They learn that if they put enough effort into something, they can achieve what they value most—recognition, admiration and a sense of being able to learn and do something they never thought possible.

A teacher lives out her school career hoping to kindle a fire in just a few of the many students who pass through the classroom. To realize that one has made a true contribution by influencing others to become the best they can be is a joy that keeps a teacher going. To accomplish this for an entire class of children, year after year, through a single project is simply too good to be true. Yet that is what a Broadway musical has done for my students over the last sixteen years. Impossible, you say? Believe me, I have never found anything to come even close to the results achieved in this way.

In a single classroom today, one finds many children for whom English is not their first language. They struggle to learn a new basis for communication. Their parents do the same. I have seen such a struggling child become so caught up in the excitement of being in a real play on a real stage that he or she somehow summons up the courage to try out for a speaking part. For me, a child with that kind of courage should always be rewarded. The child will receive the coveted part, even though the lines number only one or two. The child feels something akin to the euphoria one must have upon climbing the highest mountain. He did it! He's on his way to being accepted in this new country of his. He can communicate in his new language, not just to a few classmates but to an audience numbering in the hundreds.

All of our children are given the opportunity to participate in the shows. Children with disabilities are no exception. Minor adaptations can make it possible for any child to be successful. Under the Americans with Disabilities Act, new schools are being built and older ones remodeled so that all facilities are wheelchair accessible. A child using a wheelchair will be a part of the play just like anyone else. We have made adjustments in scripts for children with speech and language difficulties. One student, whose learning disability made it difficult for her to remember direction, had difficulty as a member of the dance troupe. We arranged for her to wear a bracelet on her right wrist so that she would remember which way to turn during the dance. Another child, one with a physical disability, also became a capable dancer.

Hidden Benefits

What if you, the teacher, have no training in drama? What if you don't even remember ever being *in* a big play? Where do you start? This describes my feeling when I first began. A friend gave me a script of a shortened version of a past Broadway hit, and after reading it I decided to give it a try. I was not seeking all the lofty objectives cited above. I simply wanted to give my students a little enrichment through a new avenue. Children are interested in themselves, and the show seemed to be a good way to capitalize on that interest. It wasn't until I started working on the project that I began to see changes in the children, benefits that I had never before considered. Since that time, our annual fifth-grade play has grown, developed and become more sophisticated and polished each year. The final product these days equals or surpasses many high school productions in quality and depth, or so I have been told. Still, to equal other productions was never my goal. I simply wanted my students to do and be the best they possibly could, and over the last sixteen years I have found that whatever is expected of them they will achieve.

Through this experience I have learned much. The object of this book is to share that knowledge and to help you begin a project that will have effects on your children far beyond your wildest dreams.

The Classroom Teacher's Advantage

There are many children's theater organizations in this country. Why then should the classroom teacher have such phenomenal success in working with student drama? The key is the distinct advantage the teacher has. There is no one *better* able to coax a good performance out of children than their teacher. The key to working successfully with youngsters is a knowledge of the individual child's personality and ability. The teacher deals with this daily, in all types of situations, and learns to handle each child so that he or she achieves at the highest level possible. This easily transfers to drama instruction. Each child is different, and what works with one frequently will not work with another. During play rehearsals the teacher uses all the knowledge gained in the classroom to be a good director. She knows how to phrase a direction to a particular child to achieve the desired results. She knows the shy child and how to draw the best out of him. The discipline problems of an active child are handled daily in school, and the teacher uses the same techniques in after-school rehearsals.

The ego of a child this age is a delicate thing and can be easily damaged. Also, peer pressure is a powerful force with which to contend. Children may be embarrassed by something in the play that their character is expected to do or say. These things cannot be discussed with the whole group during a hectic play rehearsal. But the next day in class, the teacher has a captive audience when she needs to discuss a problem with the entire cast. She explains her interpretation of a play character, and why the character would act in a particular way or say certain words. It is much easier for a child to perform a difficult part when the child knows that her peers understand the need for doing it in the prescribed way. It is easy to save face with one's friends when one can rationalize that, "This isn't my idea. I have to do what the teacher says."

A teacher sometimes makes mistakes in handling a particular child or situation in class. The chance of making a mistake is no less in a play rehearsal. However, if a teacher unintentionally embarrasses a child, it is easy to correct that situation the next day in class. Perhaps you are too demanding or harsh in a rehearsal, and the child feels uncomfortable. Left to fester, the situation may go from bad to worse. But the next day in class, the teacher is able to show by her actions in dealing with the child that she does not think less of him because he had difficulty following directions during the play rehearsal. She might joke with him more than usual, or ask him to run an errand, thereby showing him as well as the entire group that "What happened yesterday at rehearsal is behind us and forgotten."

Co-directing with Another Teacher

I began doing plays in school working with another fifth-grade teacher. The cast included all students of both classes. We had a script of a shortened version of a Broadway musical. There were about 23 speaking parts and 10 nonspeaking parts. The other 25 children in the group would act as stage crew, props or wardrobe helpers and sing in a large chorus standing on risers at the side of the stage. I had no experience at all, but the other teacher had previously put on short plays with her students. We decided that she should be the director and I should be the assistant director. As our rehearsals progressed, there were times when I disagreed with how she might have a child say a particular line or with her stage direction. Yet I never voiced my opinions during rehearsals because I knew that a child can obey only one director. We discussed my opinions when the two of us were alone. *This is essential.* Even adult professionals would have difficulty following two directors with opposing ideas.

The next year when the other teacher transferred to another school, I decided to try a play of my own. I needed an assistant director to handle all the details that I had taken care of the year before. Mary An, a fourth-grade teacher, wanted to work with me. We would combine my fifth-grade and her fourth-grade classes for the show. She had no experience in drama and was happy to allow me free rein with directing. We spent hours discussing casting, stage directing, how to handle particular children with the greatest success and a multitude of other details. Most of this was done over the phone during the evening because our in-school hours were full.

Mary An took charge of finding costume patterns, controlling children backstage, setting up parents' meetings, organizing the program and so many other details. Because our show was a shortened version of one then being performed at a nearby community theater, she even arranged for cast members and their parents to see the play. The trip was a highlight of the entire school year. The benefit to the children of seeing a play that they were working on was immeasurable to them and to us. For the next several years we tried to arrange for each cast to see at least a semiprofessional version of their play before their performance. Finally, however, came the year when no other group was performing our show. We were forced to get along without something we had considered almost essential. And guess what! The kids did their usual masterful job in their parts! Yet who knows what might have been achieved if we'd been able to attend someone else's performance.

Perhaps seeing another version of our show had also become *my* "security blanket." I was picking up many ideas from seeing someone else's version of our show. For whatever reason, for the next 12 years we got along fine without taking the kids to see a show when one was unavailable.

That first year our show was extremely popular with our community. During rehearsals we saw that we had a real hit on our hands. We decided that our school cafeteria and tiny stage would be inadequate for the results we hoped to achieve, as well as for the size of our expected audience. We obtained permission to use the larger stage at a nearby junior high school. We decided to put on a daytime performance at our school for our student body and a second, a Friday-evening performance, for the parents and community. We included the community for two reasons. Many of the cast members and their parents had friends and neighbors who were eager to see the show, and the success of the previous year's show had generated some community interest as well. When Friday night finally arrived, we were astounded to see approximately 500 people in our audience—standing room only! Thank goodness we had moved to the larger auditorium!

The following year Mary An and I decided that we made a good team, and we would like to try another show. We both realized, however, that fifth graders are much more capable of handling a show of this type than were fourth graders. When an opening on the fifth-grade level came up in our school, Mary An requested and received that teaching assignment. By that time we had worked together long enough on the other play to trust each other's judgment, and we again produced a hit play, this time drawing an even bigger audience for our evening performance at the junior high school. We were beginning to make a reputation for ourselves, and our students were invited to perform their show for other area elementary schools. Because this involved out-of-class time, we accepted only two of the several invitations we received. Several years later, principals were calling me a year in advance in order to insure a performance at their schools.

Parent and Community Helpers

During those three years and three shows, we located some willing and talented parents to help us in all areas. During our first show, the mother of one of our students agreed to serve as our musical accompanist. We did not know at the time that she had been a voice major in college, a real bonus for us! Sandy continued to work with us for six years, appearing at all after-school rehearsals, holding before-school voice lessons with our soloists and performing miracles. One year, when her youngest child was in the show, she transposed all of the music to a lower key for our young voices. Her dedication was truly remarkable. Sandy stayed with us until her youngest child moved on to junior high school, and she took her volunteering efforts there. We understood but really missed her.

Scenery is a major part of any show. Our scenery designer has also been with us each year since the beginning. One of Jean's first projects was designing and painting a freestanding deck of a boat. A local music store owner agreed to donate a piano crate and deliver it to school free of charge. We broke it down and reassembled it to the dimensions we needed. Then Jean painted the deck of a boat on the wooden crate. The effect was superb!

Jean felt strongly that, instead of her being solely responsible for creating the scenery, the children should have an opportunity to be involved. How to accomplish this and still have it retain a professional look was the problem. She worked out a system for achieving this. It required a monumental effort on her part, but she felt it was worthwhile to enable the children to participate. Her method, described in detail in the chapter on scenery, involved creating a huge paint-by-number backdrop, with corresponding numbered cans of paint. We turned the children loose with their paint brushes, and the effect they achieved was excellent. The children took such pride in the fact that they painted the backdrop themselves, and the result was something of which they could be truly proud.

Another find among the parents that first year was a stage manager. Anne's original assignment was to control the children backstage during performances, and she did a magnificent job. As our shows became more complicated, however, so did her job. She made hats, an Indian headdress and bustle, choreographed an Indian dance, assisted with costume changes and, most important, served as a backstage counselor for nervous children. I recall one little Indian-dance soloist who was so frightened and nervous that she never would have been able to go on without Anne's support and encouragement.

The Show Goes On

During the summer after our third show, tragedy struck. Mary An, my dear friend, coteacher and assistant director, was killed in an automobile accident. After recovering from the loss of a friend and the realization of what her absence would mean to the children in our school who would never have the chance to be in the class of such a caring and excellent teacher, I began to think of the play. There was simply no way I could see that I would be able to do another show alone. I knew that there was no other teacher in the school who would be willing to undertake such a task. Mary An and I had built up the show, year after year, and it was now a very complicated procedure. It was, however, one with which we were familiar and would not have hesitated to continue. I returned to school in late August, eager as always for a new school year to start but very dejected over the loss of what had become an important part of my life—the fifth-grade play.

When I arrived at school that first day, our principal told me that an astounding thing had happened. Members of the community, parents of my former students, had been calling the school with offers to help me continue the show! If I ever needed proof that others felt our play was of as much benefit to the children as I did, here it was! One parent sent the message that not only would she help in any way she could, but she would be at every single rehearsal, just to be on call if I needed her. Barbara became the assistant director for future shows. When Anne accepted a full-time teaching job at an area high school, Barbara added stage manager to her already monumental job as assistant director. Now, 13 years later, Barbara is still on the job. Truly, the show could not have existed without her!

The day came when we had to find a musical replacement for Sandy. Sure enough, another parent stepped forward to volunteer. When she moved, we scouted around and found still another parent to fill those musical shoes. Carol was a nurse as well as a talented musician. She became so interested in working with us that she even arranged her daily nursing schedule so that she could attend all our rehearsals. That really took some doing on her part! She stayed with us for two years before her family was transferred to another state. We were desperate for a musical replacement, and we found one in our own school music teacher. Kathy had to do some major restructuring of her after-school hours in order to attend rehearsals. She worked on show music during regular music classes and was on hand at almost all rehearsals. On the days it was simply impossible for her to attend, we all pulled together to cover for her. The kids sang without music, the dancers rehearsed to an audio tape, and although it wasn't an ideal arrangement, it was the best we could do. Kathy was truly a lifesaver for volunteering; after all, how can one put on a musical production without music? She became our musical director and did a great job.

Jean, the scenery designer and our genius-in-residence, in addition to designing the scenery, appeared at countless rehearsals, looking for props we needed for the show. She always managed to find or make them. Would you believe a butter churn made from ice-cream containers and a broom handle? (The high school drama department even borrowed that one.) How about ice-cream cones made of Styrofoam and cardboard? Her husband even got into the act by becoming our cast photographer, building flats so we could have more scenery changes, donating and then wiring lights for the stage and so much more.

There never seemed to be a shortage of volunteers. Before she moved clear across country with her family, Judy helped to choreograph and teach dances to children who'd never before danced a step. Mary, our school principal, was a magician at cutting red tape and made our shows better in a hundred different ways. Once I found her sitting on the floor putting rubber "feet" on our small portable stage so it wouldn't slide around during active dance numbers. She recognized the public relations benefit of our show to the school, and she was one of our biggest supporters.

JoAnn, a parent who owned a printing company, offered to have our programs professionally printed at no cost to us! She really enjoyed working with us and the children and wanted to become even more involved. The following year she became our costume coordinator, researching period costumes and locating patterns that could be adapted to our needs. She served as chair of the Costume Committee, seeing that costumes were made for those children whose parents were not able to sew. She created specialty costumes out of odds and ends. In short, she was a marvel we could not do without. She's still with us, 12 years later.

Bert joined us. She was so determined to contribute in some way that she began attending every rehearsal looking for ways to help. She started by standing at the back of the rehearsal hall, letting us know when a child wasn't speaking loudly enough to be heard clearly. I was impressed with her dedication, and one time I asked her to see what she could do to improve a particular child's diction. She took over the job with great enthusiasm, meeting with the child before school and arranging evening sessions by calling the parents. The child showed tremendous improvement. Year by year Bert's job grew. She was a diction coach, a part-time choreographer and a drama coach in spots that remained awkward despite my best efforts. Bert had watched me as I'd taken rehearsal time from the entire group to try and work through the problem, with no success. She then used what she'd seen me do and spent hours with a child or children in private, working until all was perfect. During rehearsals, she was now a backstage supervisor, keeping excited children quiet. She saved me many a headache!

Jeanne, a mother who had helped backstage when her child had performed in a past play, called to volunteer again. She was stationed on one side of the stage, and Barbara took the other side. Jeanne was responsible for overseeing our lights technician and also for the children who entered or exited from her side of the stage. She was always cool and calm except for the day when she was busy with something else and a nonspeaking actor, bent on mischief, stuck a paper clip into an electrical outlet. We'll *never* know why he wasn't killed outright! The only result was that he blew out every fuse in the school. Truly, our guardian angel was watching over us that day!

So our play not only continued but grew and blossomed. Production is ideal when two teachers work together but not impossible to do with one, especially with the help of so many wonderful and talented people. Each one has his or her own specialty, and each one has been caught up in the fun of working with children, expecting much from them and finding that they do not let you down. After Barbara's first year as assistant director, she said to me, "You know, I would *pay* to be allowed to do this!"

This book is for you even if you aren't a teacher. The most necessary ingredient in an undertaking such as this is a love of working with children. If you have that and want to try a play with your group, ages 9 through 13, be they scouts, church youth or some other, we encourage you to do so. A teacher may have the advantage of knowing her children better than you do yours, yet the results you will be able to achieve will still surpass anything else you've ever tried. So, if you have an interest, a desire and a love of children, we are happy to share with you all of the tricks we have learned in the past sixteen years. Oh, how we *hope* that you will have as much fun as we do!

2

Choosing and Adapting a Script

If you plan to do a play during the school year, summer vacation is the ideal time to look for a script. The first prerequisite to consider in choosing a script is appropriateness for children. Because Broadway musicals are aimed primarily at adult audiences, almost every story will have parts that must be eliminated, ranging from profanity to murder. In addition, most original scripts are designed for a finished play length of at least two hours. Because this is an extremely difficult length for young children (though it has been done), you should consider shortening the original. There are also parts of a story line that move slowly and are, therefore, boring to children. These parts are best eliminated. Even plays aimed at general audiences will have some parts better left out.

It is also necessary to scale down the love interest in a Broadway musical. The most you can expect from 9- to 13-year-olds is to hold hands at the moment in an adult performance where you would expect a kiss. Children are shy with members of the opposite sex and even hand-holding is difficult for them. Be aware of this in rehearsals. It requires special handling from you.

What Makes a Script Suitable?

Here's an example of how I adapt an original script for fifth graders. Notice that I do not change words; I simply omit inappropriate ones.

Scene: Barnyard. Two cowboys meet.

Uncensored Version

DICK: Hey, Joe, what's a horny fella like you doin' out here sittin' in the damn mud on a Saturday night?

JOE: My girl, Crazy Beverly, has hitched herself up to that jackass Winston and gone to the square dance.

DICK: Well, don't just sit there. Let's steal ourselves a couple a' these fartin' ponies and go down to the Hot and Heavy Saloon for some wicked whiskey to drown your sorrows.

JOE: Hot damn! We'll do it!

Cleaned Up Version

DICK: Hey, Joe, what's a fella like you doin' out here sittin' on a Saturday night?

JOE: My girl, Beverly, has hitched herself up to Winston and gone to the square dance.

DICK: Well, don't just sit there. Let's go down to the saloon.

JOE: We'll do it!

Another important prerequisite of the preferred script is the number of speaking and nonspeaking parts available. Most children want to perform on stage, so a large cast is important. I prefer plays that have at least 25 speaking parts and several nonspeaking parts (a crowd scene works wonders). Few Broadway plays, however, use large numbers of actors. Professionals must be paid, and that adds to the cost of producing a play. You do not have this problem. In fact, yours is just the reverse. You *need* speaking parts.

I always make up a list of all the characters and note how many lines each person speaks throughout the entire play. The entire auditions committee gets a copy of this list. If one child does better than another in auditions, that child is given the part with the most lines. This list is a particularly valuable tool in casting minor parts.

When deciding which songs to include in your shortened version of a show, you would be wise to find out which songs are published in the vocal selections book for your show. All Broadway shows have published songs in such books. They are available from any music store that carries a wide variety of sheet music. You will find that not all of the songs from your play are in this vocal selections book. If you have your heart set on a particular song not in the book or on separate sheet music, you will have to order the full musical score for the show through the music store. It may cost four to eight times as much as the vocal selections book and could take up to two months to arrive. You will save yourself time and money by including in your play only those songs in the vocal selections book.

A simple costume, but perfect for the part of Dorothy in *The Wizard of Oz*.

Your next consideration should be the scenery requirements for the play. Try to have no more than two or three different scenery locations and repeat those for various scenes. In one production we planned to have a train scene because it is easy to portray. The original script called for a later scene to take place aboard a boat, although the location was not essential to the story. For our show we simply changed the boat to a train and thus eliminated the necessity for another stage set. Be sure to read the chapter on scenery before you make your final decision on a script. I have filed away several appealing scripts simply because we have not yet figured out how to handle the scenery required. Perhaps someday we will have the expertise to try them.

Costumes are not a major consideration in choosing a script. Although costumes are very important to the success of a show, most problems they present are easy to solve. Parents are quite willing, with direction and suggestions from you, to provide stage clothing for their children. They want their youngsters to shine too. Rodgers and Hammerstein's *The King and I* would require more in the way of planning and showy fabrics than would their play *Oklahoma!*, which uses outfits from the American West.

Script Sources

Where will you find suitable scripts? The public library is an excellent source because many plays have been published and are readily available. Other play scripts are available from specialized libraries that also handle licenses to perform those shows. Most will loan you a script to read and consider. When you write to them, ask for a libretto, which is the dialogue of the play and the lyrics of the songs. Purchase the music after you have decided on your play, or wait for it to arrive with your rented material. I usually needed mine early, so I also purchased a vocal selections book. The following list includes those libraries most likely to handle plays you will be considering. Most of them will send, free of charge, lists of plays they control.

(1) Rodgers and Hammerstein Theater Library
    598 Madison Avenue, New York, NY 10022
(2) Music Theater International, Inc.
    545 Eighth Avenue, New York, NY 10018
(3) Tams Whitmark Music Library, Inc.
    560 Lexington Avenue, New York, NY 10022

Read through the libretto and decide what you are going to omit to simplify production. A show of 75 to 90 minutes is best. We have omitted songs and sometimes parts of songs that were too long, too complicated or unsuitable for children. Also, many librettos designate minor characters as simply Man, Woman, Boy or Girl. Young children need their characters to have names. I have, therefore, given each such character a name. This in no way changes what that character says in the play. It only gives the child a name with which to identify his part. Many of our children have their stage names printed on T-shirts, an indication of the names' importance to them.

When you have chosen your play, write the licensing agency again, requesting a contract. They also rent music and dialogue material to their licensees. There is a fee for the license and also a fee for rental of materials. You must also make a refundable deposit for these rented materials. The licensing fee varies, depending on several things, among them the admission fee you charge for your show and the seating capacity of your auditorium.

The Importance of Minor Roles

The children who have minor speaking parts or nonspeaking parts must be made to feel important to the overall success of the show. A technique that I have used in almost every show is to create a simple dance production number, involving 18 to 24 children. Once we had an Indian dance involving 19 children. One of these was the drummer who sat at the front corner of the stage and maintained a steady beat on a small drum in time with the music. Our drummer felt (and *was*) very important! Our dancers and drummer wore identical costumes. They were a real hit in the show. More important, they felt essential to its success! The dance became such a significant segment of the show that some of the children with major parts who were not in the dance were actually envious of those minor characters who were!

Another logical place for a routine involving many children is the finale. We like to end our shows with a flamboyant number. The children who have minor parts are used in a dance or marching-type sequence, and they end up in lines across the stage with an aisle down the middle. Then the lead characters walk through that center aisle and form a front row. The "star" of the show is the last one to walk through the aisle and is, therefore, automatically placed in the center of the front row. This is always a musical number, and the entire cast is on stage, singing their hearts out at the final curtain. It always brings a roaring applause from the audience.

The last chore before the script is complete is to divide it into 10 to 12 sections. Those divisions do not necessarily fall according to scenes. Some scenes are far too long to practice in one session, particularly in the beginning. I try to divide the sections according to cast requirements. Some parts of a scene deal with only a few characters and other parts with other characters. My divisions are made so that certain children stay after school one day and others another day. It seems wasteful to ask a child to stay after school to say only a

Many shows can be linked to the school curriculum.

line or two. It is better to continue rehearsal the day before until the child says his line. He may even exit the stage at that point. Then begin a new section the next day. This is not always possible, but try to do it whenever you can.

After deciding on the sections, draw a line under the last line in each section, and be sure each is numbered. These numbers are put into the Rehearsal Schedule so the children will know which sections of the script are to be practiced on a particular day. The Rehearsal Schedule lists which sections are to be practiced on which days. I also list those sections on the chalkboard daily, as part of our school-day academic schedule. There is no excuse for anyone missing a rehearsal!

3

Finances and Organization

During the summer months you have reviewed many scripts and chosen the one you will use this year. You have decided which portions to omit because they are inappropriate for children.

Where Does the Money Come From?

It is now time to consider how to finance your show. For your maiden voyage on the sea of Broadway plays the major resources and supplies will come from your school. I certainly do not mean that you should go to your principal and ask for an allocation of money for your project! No matter how supportive your principal is, he or she would have to turn you down. School systems operate on tight budgets, and financing plays is not at the top of their list of essentials. Most schools do provide a certain amount for art supplies for the students. You will probably find a roll of white butcher paper in your building. Cut into lengths, taped together and painted with school tempera paint, it will make a serviceable backdrop. Painting a backdrop is a class art project—and a good one! For our schedules and programs, we began by using school paper and copying machine.

Next you will draw on another resource: the parents of your students. They will always be happy to provide the costumes their children need if the costumes are reasonably priced and each child does not require too many changes of clothes. Most of our young actors need only one costume per play. Only the leads may require more, and that never presents a problem. The parents of the main characters, being proud mommas and papas, are usually willing to make a larger investment in costumes than those of the minor characters. That is to be expected and the main characters are always the ones with the most costume changes. So, costumes are not a financial problem for you.

In addition to costumes, parents often can provide other things you need, such as makeup, props and lights. Our makeup was donated that first year by mothers who gave us unwanted shades of powder, rouge and lipstick. Someone always has scrap lumber on hand and may be willing to donate it for scenery. We borrow most of our props. Basements and attics are gold mines to someone involved in play production. Check yard or garage sales for items that cannot be borrowed. Expand your search by putting a notice of items needed in the PTA newsletter that goes home to the parents of all the children in school. You'll be amazed at the cooperation you receive!

The only other source for your first show is *you*. Every teacher spends his or her own money in the classroom because of school systems' tight budgets. I have learned to ration the other classroom expenditures and save my resources for the play. In terms of the benefit to my students, this play ranks near the top of the list and therefore is worthy of my money. Each profession has its business expenses, and the play is mine. I have never regretted a single penny put into it. Lest you be uneasy as to how much money you will need to spend, let me reassure you. My only real expense that first year was for the film and developing for our show snapshots. That consisted of about three rolls of film—not an unreasonable outlay!

Our first shows were not as expensive to produce as later ones. We try to make each show better than the one before, hence, the increase. Also, one tends to spend according to the resources available. I hesitate to quote exact figures; prices fluctuate from year to year. Yet I want to stress that you should never hesitate to undertake a project because of financial considerations. "Where there is a will there is a way!" It can be done without selling advertisements in your program and without charging an admission fee, which is the way most high schools finance their dramatic productions. When the community sees your first show, they will be impressed! Consequently, next year's parents will be willing to do more for you. Our PTA immediately recognized the worth of what we were doing. I had volunteered to serve as faculty representative to the PTA Board during the second year of our play, so I was present to answer questions when individual members asked. When they heard that I was financing part of the play out of my own pocket, they immediately rushed to my aid with offers of financial support. At first the amount of money was small, but as shows became more sophisticated and expensive, amounts increased.

It has been reported to me following the first edition of this book that at least one teacher found that his PTA Board tried to assume partial control over the show in direct proportion to the amount of financial support given. This group even went so far as to try and dictate the choice of show. *This has never happened to us.* The only thing about the play discussed in PTA Board meetings was projected show cost. No other aspect of the production was mentioned at all. If it had been, I would simply have said, "We will consider your suggestion."

Our PTA has always been our most staunch supporter, giving money but leaving the rest completely to us. They have always been a truly wonderful, cooperative group of people, and we could not have accomplished what we did if this had not been the case. I have nothing but praise for every phase of my association with them.

Our first step into bigger expenditures came in the area of scenery. We bought large rolls of backdrop paper, rather than working with the school's narrower butcher paper. We also purchased lumber and constructed several flats. See chapter 10, "Scenery," for more information on this subject.

During our first show, our lights consisted of borrowed spotlights attached to an old board. For later shows we were able to purchase secondhand lights and make a permanent installation on a homemade light frame. The wiring and switches did cost money. Eventually a volunteer constructed and wired a complete set of portable footlights, probably the single greatest improvement in our lighting setup that we ever achieved.

Another purchase one year was a headdress kit for Chief Sitting Bull in our show. We found a parent who was willing to put it together for us—no easy task! We also purchased economical feathered headband kits for all our Indian dancers. We retained the Chief's headdress for future use, but we let the dancers keep theirs. They cost only $1.25 each.

As our financial resources increased, so did our picture taking. For our first show we took three rolls of film. For our latest one we took eight rolls. Some pictures never turn out as well as you would like, and our volunteer photographer was determined to document our wonderful show with plenty of good snapshots. Also, he somehow managed to get every single child in at least one picture, even the stage crew when they took a bow at the end of the show. When the children ordered and paid for almost a thousand prints, we knew they felt as we did. Later, two students from an area high school vocational program came to our evening performance with a video camera, taped the show, and then made copies of the videotape for any parents who wanted to purchase them.

If we had more money, I am sure we would find a way to use it. Yet today our shows are quite elaborate, and our audiences probably think they are expensive to produce. The financial load is shared by so many that it is a burden to no one. We really prefer to borrow items whenever possible rather than to buy them. When we do buy something, we then have a storage problem. You always accumulate a few things for each show, and as the years roll by, these things add up to quite a collection. There is only a tiny space in our school to store equipment such as scenery, lights, extra costumes, props (that butter churn, for example), etc., and so my basement at home is becoming crowded.

The Parents' Meeting

September is busy with the beginning of a school year. Teachers have no time to be actively involved in play production. In your role as classroom teacher, you are constantly assessing your students, their interests, abilities and personalities. You use this information in your daily job of being their teacher. Without knowing it, you are also mentally storing information that will be useful to you in casting a play and in developing realistic characters.

As October rolls around, you will begin to think of the play. One of your first jobs is to tap the talents of the parents. Send home a letter detailing the fact that you will endeavor to put on a Broadway musical in collaboration with your students. Stress that, although the children will be the actors, at their age they cannot be expected to handle alone all the backstage details necessary to a successful play—and you are aiming for a smashing success! You emphasize that this will be a project involving primarily after-school hours. *No academics will suffer because of the play!* This project is *extra* enrichment!

In your letter tell them the name of the play and the fact that all children who participate in auditions will be guaranteed a speaking part. Mention that *each* child will participate, whether on stage or behind the scenes. Do not even consider the child who does not *want* to participate. I have never found a single youngster in that category, and I have now spent many years in this venture!

The key phrase in your letter is, "An undertaking of this size is impossible without much parent help." List some of your needs, such as a Costume Committee, scenery designer and painting supervisors, a makeup crew to apply makeup to between 30 and 50 children's faces, and so on.

Every situation will have its own set of special requirements. The folding stage and cafeteria in our school were far too small for our cast and for the size of our anticipated audience. We sought permission to use the nearby junior high school stage and auditorium. Consequently, we needed to practice on that stage a few times. We had to have parent drivers willing to transport children to and from the junior high school for three rehearsals. If we performed for other area elementary schools, parent volunteers were needed to transport children, scenery and props. Adjust your list to suit your particular needs.

We were overjoyed when the county later renovated our school, adding a gymnasium with a combination music room/stage attached. This meant no more hauling scenery and children, as the gym was big enough for our community audience, and other schools could bring their students to our school on performance day if they so desired.

My letter to the parents of my students goes something like this.

Dear Parents,

We have decided to try something new this year!!!! How would you react to the idea of your child participating in a shortened version of a real Broadway play? I am convinced that such an undertaking is possible for fifth grade students, and the children agree with me! We have decided to perform *Annie Get Your Gun*, music and lyrics by Irving Berlin, book by Herbert and Dorothy Fields. The children are very enthusiastic about the project and look forward eagerly to getting the production under way. Much advanced preparation will be required, however, including obtaining help from our parents.

Every single child in the fifth grade will have an opportunity to participate in our show, whether on stage or behind the scenes. We will hold auditions in late November, and rehearsals will begin when we return from the winter vacation. We plan to present our show to our parents and members of the community in early April, just before spring vacation. We have allowed this length of time to work on the play because it will be almost entirely an after-school activity. We plan to use very little classroom time, so that no child's academic progress will suffer as we work on our show. School is our first priority. This other activity, however, will be enriching for the children. They are very excited about it, as am I!

An undertaking of this size would be impossible without much parent help. We would like to hold a parents' meeting on Monday, October 15, in the library of Cedar Park School for the purpose of organizing committees, discussing costumes, props, scenery, etc. We would appreciate your support and ideas at that meeting if you are able to attend. Please fill out the attached form if you are able to help us, and return it to school with your child. Please check more than one category if possible.

PLEASE FILL OUT THIS FORM AND RETURN IT TO SCHOOL.

I *(will, will not)* be able to attend the parents' meeting on Monday, October 15, at 7:30 P.M. in the school library.

I *(will, will not)* need help from the Costume Committee in making my child's costume. (This Costume Committee will assist those parents who are unable to sew.)

I am interested in helping with the following:

_____Musical Accompanist
_____Scenery Designer
_____Costumes
_____Makeup
_____Transportation of children and equipment to other schools
_____Dance helpers (helping children to learn dances)
_____Supervisors for children painting scenery (Please send in 1 lb. coffee cans with plastic lids for paint. We are collecting *now.*)
_____Backstage supervision of children during dress rehearsals and performances
_____Typing and Program
_____Carpentry (we need someone to build us a simple flat on which to hang scenery)
_____Cast Photographer
_____Cast party (organizing refreshments and room decorations)
_____Other (specify)

Child's name_____
Parent signature_____

At the meeting, begin by telling the parents about the plans you have already made. This is to be a joint teacher-child-parent effort, and parents have a right to be kept informed on all details. *Be sure to let your enthusiasm show!* There's one thing about enthusiasm: it's very contagious! If the parents are excited about the play, your job will be much easier. Then begin recruiting. You already have the forms the parents filled out and returned to school, so you know the areas in which you need additional help.

If your play is a musical and your school music teacher cannot serve as your accompanist, your first task is to find a competent and dedicated parent who will fill this role. This is perhaps the *most difficult position* to fill because that person will be needed at almost all rehearsals for three months. If no one volunteers, tell them that without an accompanist there can be no show. They certainly don't want to see this happen, so someone will volunteer.

Next you'll need someone to help you with the scenery. The finest play in the world lacks something special without the proper scenery. Prior to the meeting ask your students whose parents are artists. Weekend painters may be too shy to volunteer this information, but your students may be able to give you a lead. I found Jean, a talented artist, among my parents during the meeting for the first play I ever produced. She has been with the show ever since, and has been able to come up with ideas for scenery to fit the most complicated situations. The magic of her talent is demonstrated best when one sees how a single backdrop can be adapted to several totally different settings. Be sure to study the chapter on scenery, where her ideas are explained and illustrated.

If you are co-directing with another teacher, your assistant director will probably serve as stage manager also. If you are directing solo, find two or three patient and confident souls who can withstand the rigors of disciplining excited children backstage while assisting with costume changes, props, scenery, lights, curtain and any unexpected problems.

The next thing you need is a volunteer to head each committee. The costume chairman and her committee of seamstresses are in charge of making costumes for any child whose parent cannot sew. For our production of *Annie Get Your Gun* this committee was responsible for 19 Indian dancers' costumes. They purchased and cut out the fabric from a master pattern. The fabric pieces and sewing directions were sent home with every dancer whose parent was able to sew the costume. The others were made by the committee.

Another year the committee brought sewing machines to school one evening and, in assembly-line fashion, put together six dresses made from the same pattern but in different colors. One person sewed darts, another did seams and someone else was in charge of ruffles or collars. It worked very well, and we had fun doing it together. The "Costumes and Makeup" chapter will give you ideas.

The makeup chairperson's job is to call the members of the makeup crew and schedule them to work before each dress rehearsal and performance. Be sure to have your makeup chairperson read the chapter "Costumes and Makeup."

Do you need a choreographer? Each of our plays has had at least one dance in it, and many have had two or more. An adult with dancing experience can do the job *if* she is used to working with children. Interestingly, the nondancing adult has an advantage over the professional. She does not have a head full of ideas for dances that could easily become too complicated for children. Someone who knows less about dance will probably be able to come up with steps more in line with the ability of untrained children. We have used both experienced and inexperienced dancers with equal success.

If you have no one willing to make up a dance, try it yourself. It isn't difficult, and others may be willing to teach the dance once it is planned. There are several basic steps that are easy for children, and they are described in the chapter on dance. Once I had a student in my class who was a fine ballerina. She was thrilled when I asked her to choreograph a short dance number for three little girls. She even persuaded her dance teacher to help.

Each show has its own requirements in the way of props. Many unusual needs can be filled at the parents' meeting. One year we needed a saddle that was light enough for a ten-year-old child to carry. A parent volunteered to borrow a pony saddle for us. Another parent located two Indian blankets and real farm tools.

At parents' meetings we have found a volunteer who would handle our programs for us, a volunteer to head a committee to plan the cast party and a chairperson for our Transportation Committee who would call drivers whenever we needed them. Every show needs a little carpentry. Look for a volunteer who enjoys woodworking. We also located a father who had an excellent camera to serve as our cast photographer—a very important job. He even took off work on Dress Rehearsal Day to take pictures of the show so that he could move freely in front of the stage and not have to worry about an audience getting in his way and vice versa. He still works with us, also taking pictures at our evening performances and candid shots behind the scenes.

Sometimes you find help in areas you haven't considered. We discovered a father who had done some drama in college. He offered to work with any children who had special problems. He became our diction coach in the years before Bert joined our team. There are always a few diction problems when working with children. He worked with youngsters at his house on evenings and weekends. I gave him one very special challenge. A tall, beautiful, very feminine girl was playing the part of an Indian chief. I asked our diction coach to teach her how to act like a man. He blinked, he gulped, he thought, and he did it! I'll never know how.

In addition to getting volunteers for all those little jobs that you will never have time to oversee, you accomplish another purpose with your parents' meeting. You let them see that an undertaking such as a Broadway show is not impossible, even for ten-year-old children. They catch your enthusiasm, and this is of the utmost importance to you. There will always be a few parents willing to do the minimum required, but you will find many more who will be the backbone of your show. They will have so much fun that they may volunteer to help you again the next year, even though they have no child in fifth grade. You will learn whom to call when an unforeseen problem arises—those always willing to take on one more job.

Presenting the Script

By early November your students are eager to begin work on the play. Give each child a script. Caution the children that this is the only script they will be given. I always staple every script into a manila folder, and on the front I put the name of the play and the name of the child to whom it belongs. This small expense is worthwhile. The children are proud of their scripts, and the folder helps them keep everything together.

After the children have had the scripts for about a week, we hold a cast meeting. I read the script aloud while they follow along silently. We discuss the story, who each character is and how he or she would act. We discuss the scenes and any confusing lines. The children may not understand some of the humorous lines, either because of unfamiliar idioms or because of the sarcasm used by the character.

This is also the time to talk about the love interest in the play and how it is handled in the script. Inform the children that if they cannot handle the "mushy" lines, they should not try out for those parts. The most that I have been able to achieve with children of this age is hand-holding. One script required the lead characters to dance a waltz together. A lack of experience in ballroom dancing made the children look awkward—all feet. They managed, though, and the audience understood. Some children are simply unwilling to try, and they should not audition for a part they cannot handle. When actually rehearsing those scenes in later months, if a child resists hand-holding, for example, I remind him of the commitment made when he auditioned for that part. All children know of the requirements of the various parts from the beginning, and in accepting a part they agree to perform what is required.

The next step is to send home a letter with the children to inform their parents of the audition date and the costume requirements for each part. Generally the leads need more costumes than do the lesser parts. Parents have a right to know what costumes will be necessary for particular parts before the children audition. The letter may include either descriptions or pictures to illustrate our costume ideas.

Included in that letter should be a rehearsal schedule. We hold all dramatic rehearsals after school, and each lasts a minimum of 45 minutes. (See "Rehearsals," Chapter 5.) During the second month of rehearsals, we extend the time to one hour because we practice larger portions of the play at each rehearsal. During the week before our performance, when we practice the entire play every day, it usually takes us 1½ hours a day. We realize this isn't easy on the children after a full day at school. However, they are so excited because our first performance is only a week away that I do believe they'd do whatever I required, no matter what.

We have never had a single complaint. Not even from those children who have other activities planned for their free time. The play always comes first. Because the lead characters are usually required at most if not all rehearsals, children who have a heavy after-school schedule of piano or dance lessons or athletic activities, are not encouraged to try out for a major part.

One year I had a talented little girl who was heavily committed to various after-school activities. There were times when she even had difficulty keeping up with her schoolwork. Yet her mother encouraged her to try out for the female lead in the play. As her teacher I could see, perhaps better than her mother, that the child would simply be unable to cope with another big undertaking. She was assigned a lesser part. She gave an excellent performance, and the relief that she felt at not receiving a major part was evident in class. She was a much happier youngster than she would have been otherwise, and the decision was not hers. She could save face at home because the *teacher* had not placed her in the lead part. If I had not worked closely with this child in the classroom, I would not have known the pressure she was under from other activities, and I might have given her the lead. This would have made an already hectic schedule worse for her. As things turned out, I had a happy child, able to cope with what was expected of her.

Seeing a Professional Show

Another activity that should be mentioned in your early November letter to the parents is the possibility of taking interested children to see a professional version of their play before they are called upon to perform it. Many years we have been fortunate in locating a local theater producing our show. We always charter a bus for the trip. One year when no local group was doing our play, we went to a city 100 miles away, where a theater group was performing it. We had a wonderful time! A dinner theater or community playhouse is usually within the price range of most families.

It is very valuable for the children to have an opportunity to see their play done by someone else. First, the scheduling of a cast activity like that seems to draw the children into a cohesive unit, besides giving all of us a wonderful evening together. Also, I believe the children are better able to perform the parts of their characters after watching adults do it. One year we arranged to see a play *before* we held our own auditions. As it turned out, the children did not know whom they were to portray in our play and thus did not know which character to watch. They did not receive as much benefit from this experience as other groups who attended a show *after* our play was cast. So try to schedule such a trip in late January or February. The timing is better for the children.

I remember one year when seeing another version of our play, *The King and I*, just about saved the show. We'd cast a Korean child in the lead, as the king. He was a shy child, quiet and unassuming. As I worked with him, I could not get him to act "kingly." He simply could not comprehend a concept so far removed from his own life and personality. We had a terrible time. I acted out some of his scenes for him, so he could watch, but even that didn't help. Finally we read that the Broadway cast of this play was to perform the show in a city near ours. We scheduled a trip. This child watched and absorbed every move made by the professional leading man, and at our next rehearsal his performance was indeed "kingly." In fact, I couldn't have asked for more. I was so proud of him!

Audition Announcement

Your letter to the parents may resemble this one.

Dear Parents,

The time has arrived at last when we will begin work on *The Wizard of Oz*. Auditions will be held after school on Wednesday, November 27, and Friday, November 29. The cast will be announced on Monday, December 2. The children will then have until January 2 to learn all of their lines well.

Rehearsals will begin on January 2 and will be held after school *each day* for a minimum of 45 minutes during the months of January through April 6. This show will be truly a team effort, and it is essential that each child who has a speaking part be able to participate in scheduled rehearsals. Therefore, we do not encourage a child to try out for a major part unless he has an after-school schedule that will permit attendance at required rehearsals. Every child who is in a particular scene will be expected to stay for rehearsal on the days when his scene is practiced. Please sign and return the enclosed permission slips for auditions and rehearsals.

Each child will have a part in this production, either on stage or behind the scenes. Those who participate in auditions will be guaranteed a speaking part. We also need a stage crew, prompter, and someone to operate the lights.

Enclosed is a detailed description of the costumes suggested for the various parts. If a problem arises in meeting these needs, we will be happy to adapt ideas using available materials. We are flexible because we realize that some fabrics or designs may be hard to find. Please let me know if some difficulty arises.

Also attached to this letter is a complete Rehearsal Schedule and a Master Parts Schedule. By referring to it daily, you will know whether or not your child will be attending rehearsals on that day.

We would like to take interested fifth graders to see a professional version of *The Wizard of Oz* before our performance. If you hear of a local dinner theater or drama group that will be presenting the play, please contact me. Please check with friends in other communities within a 100-mile radius of our town.

We have a very exciting time ahead of us. We wish to thank you in advance for your cooperation.

Sincerely,
Beverly Ross

My child _____ has my permission to attend auditions for *The Wizard of Oz* after school on November 27 or 29.
Signed_____

My child_____ has my permission to attend rehearsals after school during January through April 6 for *The Wizard of Oz*.
Signed_____

A sample schedule follows. The sections referred to are those marked off and numbered in the script.

Rehearsal Schedule and Master
Parts Schedule for *The Wizard of Oz*

JANUARY

Monday	Tuesday	Wednesday	Thursday	Friday
		1/ Holiday	2/ 3:15 - 4:00 Sec. 1	3/ 3:15 - 4:00 Sec. 2
6/ 3:15 - 4:00 Sec. 4	7/ 3:15 - 4:00 Sec. 3	8/ 3:15 - 4:00 Sec. 5	9/ 3:15 - 4:00 Sec. 6	10/ 3:15 - 4:00 Sec. 7
13/ 3:15 - 4:00 Sec. 4	14/ 3:15 - 4:00 Sec. 8	15/ 3:15 - 4:00 Sec. 9	16/ 3:15 - 4:00 Sec. 1	17/ 3:15 - 4:00 Sec. 2
20/ Holiday	21/ 3:15 - 4:00 Sec. 3	22/ 3:15 - 4:00 Sec. 5	23/ 3:15 - 4:00 Sec. 6	24/ 3:15 - 4:00 Sec. 7
27/ Teacher	28/ Workdays	29/ 3:15 - 4:00 Sec. 8	30/ 3:15 - 4:00 Sec. 9	31/ 3:15 - 4:00 Sec. 1

FEBRUARY

Monday	Tuesday	Wednesday	Thursday	Friday
3/ 3:15 - 4:00 Sec. 4	4/ 3:15 - 4:00 Sec. 2	5/ 3:15 - 4:00 Sec. 3	6/ 3:15 - 4:00 Sec. 5	7/ 3:15 - 4:00 Sec. 6
10/ 3:15 - 4:00 Sec. 4	11/ 3:15 - 4:00 Sec. 7	12/ 3:15 - 4:00 Sec. 8	13/ 3:15 - 4:00 Sec. 9	14/ 3:15 - 4:00 Sec. 10
17/ Holiday	18/ 3:15 - 4:15 Sec. 1-2	19/ 3:15 - 4:15 Sec. 3-4	20/ 3:15 - 4:15 Sec. 5-6	21/ 3:15 - 4:15 Sec. 7-8
24/ 3:15 - 4:15 Sec. 4	25/ 3:15 - 4:15 Sec. 9-10	26/ 3:15 - 4:15 Sec. 1-2	27/ 3:15 - 4:15 Sec. 3-4	28/ 3:15 - 4:15 Sec. 5-7

MARCH

Monday	Tuesday	Wednesday	Thursday	Friday
2/ 3:15 - 4:15 Sec. 8-10	3/ 3:15 - 4:15 Sec. 1-2	4/ 3:15 - 4:15 Sec. 3-4	5/ 3:15 - 4:15 Sec. 5-7	6/ 3:15 - 4:15 Sec. 8-10
9/ 3:15 - 4:15 Sec. 1-2	10/ 3:15 - 4:15 Sec. 3-4	11/ 3:15 - 4:15 Sec. 5-7	12/ 3:15 - 4:15 Sec. 8-10	13/ 3:15 - 4:30 Sec. 1-5
16/ 3:15 - 4:30 Sec. 6-10	17/ 3:15 - 4:30 Sec. 1-5	18/ 3:15 - 4:30 Sec. 6-10	19/ 3:15 - 4:30 Sec. 1-5	20/ 3:15 - 4:30 Sec. 6-10
23/ 3:15 - 4:30 Sec. 1-5	24/ 3:15 - 4:30 Sec. 6-10	25/ 3:15 - 4:30 Sec. 1-5	26/ 3:15 - 4:30 Sec. 6-10	27/ 3:15 - 4:30 Sec. 1-10
30/ 3:15 - 4:30 Sec. 1-10	31/ 2:00 - 4:00 Sec. 1-10			

APRIL

Monday	Tuesday	Wednesday	Thursday	Friday
		1/ 2:00-4:00pm Sec. 1-10	2/ 2:00-4:00pm Sec. 1-10	3/ 1:00-2:00pm **Costumes & Makeup** 2:00 - 4:00 pm **Dress Rehearsal & Cast Photos**
6/ 1:00-2:00pm **Costumes & Makeup** 2:00 - 4:00 pm **Dress Rehearsal**	7/8:00-9:00 am **Costumes & Makeup** 9:15 - 10:35 am **Performance for School**	8/ **No Rehearsal**	9/6:30-7:30 pm **Makeup** 7:30 pm **Performance for Community**	10/6:30-7:30 pm **Makeup** 7:30 pm **Performance for Community** 9:00 pm **Cast Party**

(Names in parentheses do not attend rehearsal until March 3)

Section 1: Dorothy
Aunt Em
Joe
Uncle Henry

Section 2: Dorothy
Glenda
Mayor
Munchkin #1
Munchkin #2
Munchkin #3
Munchkin #4
Munchkin #5
Munchkin #6
Munchkin #7
Munchkin #8
Munchkin #9

Section 3: Dorothy
Glenda
Mayor
Munchkin #8
Munchkin #9
(All Munchkins)

Section 4: Munchkin Dancers
(All Munchkins)

Section 5: Dorothy
Wicked Witch
Mayor
Scarecrow

Section 6: Dorothy
Wicked Witch

Scarecrow
Tinman
Mayor
Munchkin #7
(All Munchkins)

Section 7: Dorothy
Scarecrow
Tinman
Lion
Wizard
Lord Growlie
Oz Lady
Man of Oz
(Citizens of Emerald City)

Section 8: Dorothy
Scarecrow
Tinman
Lion
Wicked Witch
1st Witch
2nd Witch

Section 9: Dorothy
Scarecrow
Tinman
Lion
Wizard
Servant
(Citizens of Emerald City)

Section 10: Entire Cast

An example of costume illustrations for *Annie Get Your Gun* follows:

Costume Suggestions for *Annie Get Your Gun*

Annie

Annie

Annie

Frank

Indian
dancer

Minnie,
Jessie

Jake

Dolly

An example of costume *descriptions* for the show *Annie* follows.

Annie: old, tattered outfit, old sweater (maybe with holes in it), a nice dress, a coat styled to the 1930s (maybe with a fur collar), and the classic red dress one thinks of with Little Orphan Annie.

Miss Hannigan: an out-of-style dress (perhaps a wild print), knee-high stockings rolled down to the ankle, a string of very long beads, a sweater, coat or cape, feather boa, and a cheap bathrobe and slippers. A hair net should be worn with the robe and slippers.

Warbucks: a dark suit, white dress shirt, dark bow tie, and dark shoes (not sneakers). Also a sport coat as a change of costume. (If the child does not have these items, we suggest borrowing them or looking in a thrift shop for them.)

Grace (Warbucks' secretary): a suit, a stylish party dress, a cape or coat, hat, and purse.

Rooster (Miss Hannigan's brother): two cheap sport coats, one pair of pants, shirt, tie, and hat.

Lily (Rooster's girlfriend): a dress in a wild, garish print or a solid color, a black feather boa, a purse, and a wig.

Orphans (can be girls or boys): clothes made out of identical fabric and identical pattern, one for girls and one for boys. (Chosen by the costume coordinator).

Drake (Butler in Warbucks' mansion): black pants, black vest, white dress shirt, black bow tie.

Mrs. Pugh (servant in Warbucks' mansion): dark print dress, white apron.

Mrs. Greer (servant in Warbucks' mansion): dress, white apron, hat to match those of the other servants (except Mrs. Pugh, who wears none).

Women servants in Warbucks' mansion: dark skirt, white blouse with high neck, white apron, hat.

Apple Seller: old, tattered coat, perhaps an old hat, gloves with some fingers cut out, shoes (see note below), and carries a basket of apples.

Bundles (laundry man): shirt, pants, jacket, hat, shoes (see note below).

FBI Agents: dark suits or dark sport coat and pants, white dress shirts, dark ties, and shoes (see note below).

Artie, Sophie, Fred, Peggy, Mary, Eddie, Ira, Jane (residents of "Hooverville"): old, tattered clothing, coats, hats, gloves, shoes (see note below).

Dancers (these people are also residents of "Hooverville"): old clothing, similar to Artie, Sophie, etc. They will stand out because they'll wear special hats.

NOTE: All cast members: No one will wear sneakers, as they were not the style in 1933. If you do not have regular shoes or are unable to borrow them, you must take an old pair of sneakers and spray paint them black.

In casting the play, the audition committee tries, where possible, to take the child's preferences into consideration. Therefore, each child is asked to fill out a Part Preference Form. Send this form home with instructions for the children to ask their parents' help in completing it. Stress three important points in instructing the children on how to fill out the form:

(1) They must rank all four categories.

(2) It is advisable to agree to accept *any* part for which they are chosen. This second point must be explained to the children. If they are *not* willing to accept any part, and they don't get the part they chose as first, they have eliminated themselves from consideration for any other part. I have sometimes had a child agree to accept any part and then write in something like "except a speaking part" or "except a major part." These wishes are always honored.

(3) If you receive a small part, and are interested in doing more than one thing (perhaps nonspeaking actor and also dancer), BE SURE to mark that on the form.

Date_____ Child's signature_____

Part Preference Form

TO BE FILLED OUT BY EACH FIFTH-GRADE CHILD.

Please rank the following in order of your interest. Place a (1) by your first choice, a (2) by your second choice, and so on. BE SURE TO RANK ALL FOUR CATEGORIES!!!

Rank	Category	Other Information
( )	SPEAKING PART (You must attend auditions if you want a speaking part.)	List parts that interest you most. 1._____ 4._____ 2._____ 5._____ 3._____ 6._____
( )	NONSPEAKING PART	Do these interest you? Actor_____ Stage Crew_____ Prompter_____

( )   DANCER   (If you have had any dance
                              lessons, list the kind: ballet,
                              tap, jazz, etc.)

( )   PAINTING
        SCENERY

I (am, am not) interested in participating in more than one category.
I (will, will not) accept ANY part for which I am chosen.

Once you have received a form from *every single child*, you then make up a master chart. Mine always lists the child's name, his preferences, whether he will accept any part, and whether or not he's interested in more than one category if possible. Then I make copies, one for each member of the adult audition committee, and we refer to it many times when casting the show. It's a great help! A sample follows.

Master Part Preference Form

Child's Name	1st Choice	2nd Choice	3rd Choice	Will accept any part	Will accept more than one part	Part Given
Heather	Annie	Miss Hannigan	Grace	yes	yes	Annie
Jason	Warbucks	Rooster	Drake	yes	yes	Warbucks
Karen	Dancer	Paint scenery	Non-speaking	no	yes	Dancer Paint
Bobby	Warbucks	Rooster	Dancer	yes	yes	Dancer Paint
Sarah	Paint scenery	Non-speaking	Dancer	no	no	Paint
Sean	Rooster	Drake	Non-speaking	yes	no	Drake
John	Stage Crew	Non-speaking	Paint scenery	no	yes	Stage Crew Paint
Angie	Annie	Molly	Grace	yes	yes	Molly

Although this organizational activity may seem unnecessarily complex and time consuming, it will save time in the long run. Every child and every family will know exactly what is happening and what is expected of them. The production truly becomes a team effort.

4

Auditions and Casting

The calendar shows late November. Although you have spent months working on the play, your children have yet to be actively involved. It is now their turn. They are already excited, knowing that you have held a parents' meeting. They have their scripts in hand. As Audition Day approaches, you must explain exactly what will be expected of them. Each child will be required to read a portion of the script, about one-half a page, chosen by you and announced ahead of time. You have printed copies, so the interested children may take one home and practice it. Each will be asked to sing a solo. We always use "America" because it is well known and shows how close a child can come to singing on pitch.

As soon as you make that announcement, someone will ask whether he must sing if he is trying out for a nonsinging role. My answer has always been yes. I explain that singing shows me two things that I cannot see in any other way: (1) whether or not he can sing and (2) his "stage presence," or how he handles himself on stage. He is likely to be very nervous while he is singing, but if he still does well, he can be counted on to give a good performance in front of an audience. One year a child who tried out for a lesser part did such an outstanding job that she was chosen for the lead. This would not have been possible if she had not sung a solo during auditions.

If you have more than 20 children auditioning, schedule two audition dates, one for the boys and one for the girls. When all the boys audition on the same day it is easier to compare them, and few if any mistakes are made in casting.

Audition Judges

Which adults participate in auditions and casting? The director is, of course, the most important person in attendance. As the classroom teacher, she knows the children better than anyone else. She has spent the first three months of the school year mentally storing knowledge about each child, his capabilities and his tractability. She also is aware of the child's academic situation. When first discussing the play with the children in September or October, I always point out that a major consideration at the time of casting is whether or not a child who is chosen for an important part is able to handle the additional workload of many rehearsals while keeping up with required schoolwork. The child who is lax about turning in class assignments or homework will not receive a major part. This is an added incentive in the classroom for the child who is inclined to be negligent about homework. Motivation is thus added to the classroom situation.

In addition to the director, another essential adult at auditions is the musical accompanist. The school music teacher may take part, even if she isn't the show accompanist. She has the advantage not only of having musical training but also of knowing the children.

You need at least three adults participating in auditions. If you are working with another teacher, she is your valuable third helper. She has been storing information on her students just as you have. Her instincts are sharp and completely reliable. If you are working alone, ask your assistant director to participate. She does not know the children yet, and sometimes a completely objective view from an outsider can be very helpful. You may wish to have as many as five to seven adults present. Just remember that a large committee may have more difficulty reaching consensus than a smaller one.

It is best not to have parents of students who are auditioning on the committee. However, even that can be worked out. One year our musical director had a daughter in my class. We needed her expertise in casting our play, so she attended auditions. During the casting process when we began evaluating her child, she left the room and took no part in our discussion. Her child was a talented young lady with a lovely singing voice, and our decision was relatively easy. She could not be the leading lady because she was several inches taller than our leading man. She was cast in the part of the second female lead and did a superb job!

When Audition Day arrives, give each member of the panel a

copy of the Master Chart you made from the children's Part Preference Forms and also a Speaking and Singing Voice Evaluation sheet
so that each will be using the same rating system. Columns are wide
enough to enable you to indicate a score and a few words of comment if necessary. The rating system may use plus (+), check (✓),minus
(-) or numbers from one to five. One signifies a poor score and five
is tops.

Evaluation Sheet
Speaking and Singing Voice

Child's Name	Speaking Voice		Singing Voice	
	Volume	Expression	Volume	Pitch
Linda	loud-5	+excellent	great-5	5

Audition Day

It is wise to use a large room for auditions, perhaps the school
cafeteria or auditorium. You will be better able to judge the volume
of each child's speaking or singing voice if you are some distance from
the child. The children have been told that two things the committee
will be watching for are how loud they are and how slowly they
speak. The importance of this will be covered in the chapter "Direction."

For the reading portion of the audition, it is best for you to pre-
select the part of the script to be read by each child, generally a conversation between two characters. For this "Audition Script" I choose
lines that show drama or express emotion, such as the love scene. I
want to see not only how loudly and slowly the child speaks, as well
as the amount of expression in the voice, but also I want to see how
the child will react to this type of pressure.

Copies of the Audition Script have been given to all children
approximately two weeks before auditions, so they may practice at
home if they choose to do so. Some children practice; others do not.
This alone will give you information about how serious the child is
in wanting a part and also how hard he will work if he gets it.

The lines are the same, no matter which part the child wants. This
makes it easier for you to compare the way the children read the lines.
(I don't require that they memorize anything for auditions.) I also
achieve consistency and fairness by asking the leads from last year's

show to play the scene with each auditioning child. If each child were to read with a friend, one partner might read better than another and thereby give the auditioning child an unfair advantage. Also, it gives last year's show stars a chance to help with a small phase of the show, something they are eager to do.

In the singing portion of auditions, the one vital element to consider is *pitch*. If a child cannot sing a note played on the piano, there is probably no way anyone will be able to teach him to do so. The child who can usually sing on pitch but has an occasional lapse can usually be taught with practice. The reason we choose "America" as our audition song is that the note intervals in this song are difficult, and a child whose pitch is not good will have trouble with it. Even the unpracticed ear can hear the incorrectly sung notes. You do not want to place a child in a lead part that requires him to sing if he cannot accurately hit the notes of the songs. Not only would this reflect poorly on the show, but it would be extremely embarrassing for him. He could perhaps "talk" the words of a song, or in a large group of singers he could either sing softly or simply "mouth" the words.

The average fifth-grade child has a vocal range of approximately 12 notes, beginning with A below middle C and ranging upward. Any music in a show that has notes outside of this range will present problems, and your accompanist may have to transpose the music. So you want to find the children who have the widest ranges. The child should first be asked to sing a scale, going as high as she can and then as low as she can. The accompanist should note on the child's evaluation sheet the notes the child reached at both ends of the scale. Next, the child sings a portion of "America." Sometimes you will find a child who is not really prepared. To me, this indicates that she is less willing to spend the time in developing good singing techniques or will be slow in memorizing lines. Either one might harm the show, and this lack of effort should be given considerable weight in casting the play.

Casting the Play

After the children have had the opportunity to conquer their nerves as best they can and give their "all" in auditions, your job really begins! After all of the children have been sent home, the committee of adults meets. Casting the leads comes first. You must consider many

A girl who won a boy's part.

things. First and foremost, you must eliminate from consideration those children who have difficulty maintaining an adequate academic record in the classroom. You have told the children you would do this; stick to it! Then you must balance many other considerations. The attitude and behavior record of the child are most important. Is he able to follow directions? You certainly will be giving many in the coming months. Will she try whatever you suggest? If she is stubborn, you could add immeasurably to your difficulties. Is he a behavior problem in class? A teacher-director cannot give her full attention to a play rehearsal if she must continually discipline children. How tall is he or she? Even in elementary school it will look peculiar if your leading lady towers over your leading man. Girls of this age seem to grow more rapidly than boys.

Another major consideration is the child's singing voice. The main characters usually do most of the solo singing and must be able to sing well. I remember one little boy we thought would be dynamite in a secondary lead. Yet he had a solo in the show, and he *could not sing*! He was simply tone-deaf! We decided to gamble and hope we could teach him to "talk" his song. He was a sensation! His sparkling eyes and his desire to please conquered all. The audience loved him!

As the panel proceeds down the list of characters in the play, casting becomes easier. Academic considerations weigh less heavily. For some reason, many plays have a predominance of boys' parts and not too many for girls. We have, therefore, cast girls in boys' parts. In fact, well before auditions I point out this situation and discuss it with the children. Girls are told to consider seriously trying out for boys' parts. This creates more competition for the boys, and it takes the girls time to adjust to the idea. We have always followed the true sex of the child in casting the male and female leads, but for the rest of the parts we consider the talent of the child rather than his or her sex. The girl pictured on the previous page was sensational in her part. No one could have been better. In one of our shows a little girl played the part of a prince. When we saw a professional version of our show, it was obvious to all that our "prince" did a much better job in her part than the professional actor who played it in the theater. Boys are unwilling to accept girls' parts, so don't consider that option. Besides, you usually have enough parts for boys.

The most essential thing of all in casting is to make each child feel important. Each child who auditions must receive a speaking part, no matter how small. A child who speaks so softly that you can barely hear him can be given a line that is not essential to the progression of the story. We followed this procedure with a child who had a severe speech problem. We greatly admired his courage and silently applauded his participation in auditions. He earned his speaking part, even though it was a small one. Then I remember another child with a very expressive voice and animated manner who had a speech problem. She couldn't pronounce the *r* sound, and had difficulty with the *l*. Yet we really wanted her for a secondary lead. We adopted a simple solution. Any words she said that were difficult to understand, were changed to words she could say clearly. For example, if the word was "flowers," we simply changed it to "posies." She did a great job!

In addition to the cast, you will need a stage crew. Prior to auditions I ascertain which children are interested in this job. Four youngsters seem to be the right number for this position. They must be very responsible children, for any inattention to detail can slow the tempo of the play. An inappropriate stage setting or a misplaced prop can be a disaster. Some children simply have no desire to be actors but would love to be on the stage crew. Cast members with minor parts may serve as members of the stage crew if necessary. I always appoint the most reliable of my stage crew members to be the stage crew chief. It is his or her job to double check every single thing before giving the signal to the adult stage manager that all is ready for the scene to begin.

You will also need a lights technician. That sounds important, doesn't it? This is the only individual in the entire group who does not appear on the stage at any time. He operates all stage lights and/or spotlights. He must have a script at his fingertips so he can mark it as necessary, follow the action of a play and turn the lights on and off at the appropriate times. He does not have to attend rehearsals during the first weeks. In early March, when we begin to work on the actual stage, he must practice his job just as everyone else does.

Another essential for every play is a prompter. This child must be a good student who reads well. The prompter must be at *every* rehearsal! He or she is needed for every scene. I always stress the importance of this job before I ask who is interested. You should try, if possible, to choose a person who has no other part in the play. She cannot serve as prompter when she is acting on stage. However, if you are working with a limited number of children, it may not be possible to have a full-time prompter. You may have to choose one from your list of minor characters. In doing so, you have made still another child feel important by adding to her part. One year we did a long play with a small number of children. Each character was on stage many times. I filled my prompter requirements by using *two* prompters. Each was assigned a part of the script for which she was responsible. There was only one part of one scene when both girls appeared on stage at the same time and during that time we had to manage without a prompter. It was unavoidable, but the system worked adequately. There is a solution to every problem if you can only find it.

To make each child feel important I rely heavily on the manner in which I announce the cast. The main characters are never a worry. Their peers know the value of the lead parts, as well as the secondary leads. It is the children with only two to four lines that concern me the most, because most of them wanted big parts and voiced those desires to their friends before auditions took place. To build their importance, I make sure their names are listed several places on the cast list. I may be able to cast a child in two parts, each of whom speak two lines. To me this is as good as casting him in a single part with four lines. I always have a dance production number in my shows, and every single child with a minor part (speaking or non-speaking) is a member of that dance troupe, as many as 20 to 24 children. I usually have some type of elaborate finale where I again use all those children with minor parts. All the children in the dance and finale troupe are listed separately. The key to soothing disappointed feelings on the day the cast is announced is to give each child with a minor part the opportunity to see his name listed as many times as possible. In several shows I had a child do a tiny solo right in the middle of the dance number—the word "solo" works miracles!

Announcing the Cast

A few days after auditions are over, announce the cast. The children will be nervous wrecks from the suspense by this time, so do it as soon as possible. We try to hold auditions at the end of a week and announce the cast on Monday. The cast list includes the names of the cast, stage crew, lights technician and prompter. "Announce" is perhaps the wrong word; you surely do not do it orally. Children seem better able to handle the written word than the spoken. It seems to be more private. When my students arrive at school on Monday morning, the cast list is posted on a chart at the front of the classroom. As the children enter they immediately run to look at it and learn what their part is. The disappointments are digested in the confusion and activity that is a part of any classroom on Monday morning. I have never seen tears as a result of a cast list being posted. If a child's part is a minor one and he'd wanted a major one, he is able to salvage his pride by seeing his name listed several times. Lead characters have none of these boosts. They do not need them.

Once after the cast list had been posted, I was faced with a new problem. Three little girls, each in turn and each in private, came to me to ask why she was not chosen for the lead. My first thought was to be very careful of what I said because children this age are very sensitive. Yet I couldn't pause before I replied or they might think I was not telling them the truth. I decided that I had to be honest with them while at the same time phrasing my answer so they did not feel rejected. To the first two girls I truthfully said that they had difficulty staying on pitch while singing. I told them that this skill came to different children at different ages. As they grew and matured they might easily develop a more accurate "ear" for pitch and in future years might well be able to do a fine job of singing. Right now, while their speaking voices were loud and expressive, their singing voices just could not handle the demands of the lead part. They both accepted what I said with great understanding. I had allowed them hope that this skill might come later.

The third child had lost the lead part for an entirely different reason, one harder to explain to a ten-year-old. She had a beautiful singing voice. The reason for her casting was an intangible one, based on a feeling and observations I had made of her. It was not readily describable. Yet I had to make her understand. The play was *Annie Get Your Gun*. The lead character, Annie Oakley, was an uneducated girl from a rural area in Ohio in the 1880s. She could not even read or write at the beginning of the story. She was an incredible marksman, though socially she had never had any of the usual advantages. The child who was chosen to play Annie was an adorable little pixie with a round face and short, blonde hair. She was a typical ten-year-old with lots of bounce and sparkle. My questioning child was a taller, beautiful girl with long, dark hair and a more reserved manner. She was more sophisticated in her actions than many girls her age. I tried to answer her by explaining that she was "too classy a lady" for the part of Annie. Had we been doing a play more in keeping with her personal character, she might well have been chosen for the lead. I emphasized her talent and beauty as I talked to her. I am not sure that she understood all of what I was trying to say to her, but she accepted it with good grace. In the part she played, that of the secondary lead, she came across as an elegant, almost regal, lady—exactly the character she was portraying. The audience marveled at her beauty and bearing. She was superb in her part! I truly think that the audition panel, faced with that difficult casting decision, made the right choice on the basis of an intangible "something" that we simply felt was right.

Once the cast is announced, it is *never* changed. I have made a public commitment to each child, and I will not renege on that commitment! As soon as the child reaches home that afternoon with the news to his parents about which part he has, his parents begin to think of costumes. A broken commitment to a child would also be a broken commitment to his parents who may already be making an early investment in costumes and accessories for him. Even if once rehearsals start you find you have made a mistake in casting, you must live with it.

I remember once when we cast the male and female leads, we didn't know at the time that these two children really liked each other offstage as well as on. Things went along in great style until just before our first dress rehearsal, when the two had a fight and "broke up." The electricity and friction on stage was tangible! They could hardly bring themselves to say their lines to each other. Disaster! Finally, I had to pull them aside and severely reprimand them for allowing personal feelings to harm the entire show. I guess I made an impression because things improved to an acceptable level. Never, never deviate from that first posted cast announcement—unless you enlarge a particular part. That action produces nothing but joy, and you can live with that!

5

Rehearsals

It is now early January. The school's winter holiday is over. Your cast has spent its vacation time working on lines. I have tried two systems with children as they memorize lines. The first year or two I found that I frequently had to correct how the children said the lines. They placed different emphasis on words or phrases than an adult would. Once a child has learned a line in a particular way, it seems difficult for her to change it. So, during December I used to set up appointments with all the lead and secondary lead characters and the parents who would be working with them most often on memorizing. At the child's home during evening hours, we went over her part, line by line, while the parent listened. The child read each line, and I told her how it should be spoken. She marked her script, underlining key words and making whatever notations were necessary to help her remember how to say it. The parent listened and remembered also. Thus, when rehearsals began in January, the child was generally able to deliver her lines in the prescribed fashion, and I had to do less correcting.

As time went on and my experience grew, however, I wondered if the time spent in that way was worth it in the end. I decided to give the children a chance to memorize on their own, but I marked each script with underlining for emphasized words and other notations. This system produced good results without all the extra time and work that the previous system had required. I still occasionally had to correct or remind a child how to say a particular line, but those infrequent interruptions to our rehearsals seemed worth the time saved from the previous system.

In the beginning the most difficult rehearsals for you are when the entire cast must attend. In a crowd scene when there are many people on stage but only a few have lines, the others become restless and disruptive. It seems easier to require only those with speaking parts to attend rehearsals during January.

You have already divided the script into 10 to 12 sections. After the script was divided, you made up a complete Rehearsal Schedule listing which sections are to be practiced on which days and a Master Parts Schedule of who is in each section. Give a copy to each child. This may seem like a wasted effort to you. After all, each child can easily look at his script to determine which sections call for his presence at rehearsal. Remember the age of the children though. They *can* look, but they don't! So a printed list is the best answer. It makes things easier for the parents too. With the list and a rehearsal schedule at home and the script at school, parents can tell at a glance whether or not their child is at rehearsal. Be sure to post a copy of that list in your classroom. Mine was used by children every single day. "Do I have rehearsal today?"

See chapter 3 for a complete Rehearsal Schedule and Master Parts Schedule. The numbers represent section numbers. You will notice that when we practice the entire play in a single day, we begin rehearsals at 2:00 P.M., about an hour before school lets out. Because we do this only five times, we have our principal's blessing. If we started full rehearsal after school the children would have to stay past 5:00 P.M. This would put too much of a burden on already tired children.

Rehearsal Location

Your rehearsal hall may be a problem because most schools have limited space available. Some early rehearsals can be held in a classroom with the stage area marked with masking tape on the floor. During January and February I hold rehearsals on our tiny fold-up stage in the cafeteria. Then during March we move rehearsals to our "stage" that doubles as the music room. One wall of the room is composed of movable doors that open to the gymnasium, where the audience will be seated. Curtains hang from the back and sides of the stage. Neither location has a front curtain. At the end of each scene, our lights technician turns out the stage lights to indicate scene changes and to allow the stage crew to change sets in the darkness when necessary.

Several years ago, before our school was renovated giving us a large stage, we presented our community performance at the local junior high school. That stage was quite large and had both front and back curtains. The children had to learn to spread out on that stage and to use overhead microphones. Their entrances and exits and all other mechanics of staging remained the same as they had practiced on the tiny stage at our school.

The experience of working on two different stages with entirely different equipment was excellent training for the children, and they became quite adept at it. During those years we were usually invited to perform our show for other area schools. Because of their experience with the two vastly different stages, the children were able to adapt to unfamiliar stages without any rehearsal or a moment's hesitation. They became versatile little actors and actresses.

Nevertheless, we were overjoyed when we no longer had to hold our community performance outside of our own school. Hauling scenery, props and children had become difficult as our shows grew in sophistication. We even decided to add a second community performance to accommodate a larger audience. So my advice is to remain flexible and creative in adapting to your facilities.

Staging

One of the first things to do in rehearsal is to tell the children where to enter and exit, where to stand while on stage and how to move for each section of the play. For some reason children think they must stand still on stage while speaking. They must be taught to move while they talk, but the method of movement is important. Refer to the chapter on direction for a full discussion of staging a play.

As rehearsals progress you will need stage-floor markings. My children always stand too far back on the stage. I put a piece of masking tape across the stage near the front and tell them that they usually will do all of their speaking on or in front of that tape line. We always use tape markings for our dance routines and finale. Without them, a circle dance formation may have a sausage shape instead. If there are overhead microphones, I tape an "X" directly below each on the floor. It is much easier and looks more natural to glance at the floor than to look above your head for the mike.

Entrances and exits require special attention. If a character exits stage left and enters again in the same scene, she must enter from that same side the next time. This is especially important if your stage has no curtain around the back, behind which the children may walk unseen by the audience. It is possible to cross the stage between scenes when the lights are out, in order to enter from the opposite side, but certainly not during the same scene. My scripts always indicate which side characters enter and exit. The terms "stage left," "stage right," "upstage" and "backstage" all refer to direction as one stands on stage and faces the audience. As long as you are teaching the children about the theater, you might as well use the correct terms.

The Prompter

Your prompter must attend every single rehearsal. This child must practice his craft just as the actors do. Tell him that to be a good prompter he must *never* take his eyes off the script! The instant that he chooses to look up and watch the play action is the time that someone will miss a line. The prompter will have to find his place in his script in order to help the actor. That takes time and causes an awkward pause on stage.

The most important part of a prompter's job is the timing of the prompted word or line. There is no way you can teach this. You can only help from time to time and wait for the child to develop his own sense of timing. He must not assume too early that an actor has forgotten a line. He must wait just long enough to be sure, and yet not so long that an unnatural pause is created on the stage. He must learn how many words of a line to "feed" the actor before that person remembers the rest of what should be said and continues on his own. In other words, the prompter needs to practice! You must resist the temptation to give him too much help. He must be allowed to develop his skill by himself. By the time opening night rolls around, my prompter usually needs no script—he has unconsciously memorized every line in the entire play! Yet his script is always in his hand, and he still keeps his eyes on every line. Nerves can hit a prompter too; he just might forget a line at a critical moment, and the tempo of the play could be damaged.

The words to the songs are also the responsibility of the prompter. Four times in the past 16 years our leading lady has forgotten the words in the middle of a solo. She has stopped singing and just stood there, bewildered and terrified! Though the prompter has "fed" the words to her, she apparently has not been able to hear the prompter over the sound of the piano. What to do? Because I was sitting in the exact center of the first row in the audience and had memorized every word of every song, I was able to say the words loud enough for them to hear me. If the audience heard me, that couldn't be helped. I had to do something *immediately* to help the poor child on the stage. Only once was the child so upset that when she exited she broke down in tears, and the stage manager had to somehow calm her down before she entered again. Those backstage adults are truly miracle workers!

Keeping the Fun in Rehearsal

The director must maintain a high level of enthusiasm during all rehearsals. If you are a classroom teacher, this is difficult after a long day of education, but it is essential for the actors to have enthusiasm, and they can get it only from you. Three months of rehearsals can be an eternity to children of this age. It is your job to see that the "fun" never ends. This is easy in January because the children are excited about beginning work on the play.

February can be a long month if you allow it to be. By then the children are beginning to feel they have done their parts so often that they know every line. They could become bored and begin to be sloppy about details. I even have seen this happen with a professional Broadway actor who played the same part over and over for years. He had sloppy diction, sloppy volume, and kept his back to the audience constantly.

Do not allow this to happen in your show. What is practiced is what will be transmitted to an audience, and boredom or disinterest can also be practiced if you are not careful. This is a time when parents can be a tremendous help. Send home a letter, inviting them to attend rehearsal whenever they have the time. A child who has done an excellent job in previous rehearsals may "freeze" when Mom or Dad walks in to watch her perform. You may see many nervous gestures that were never there before. If a parent's presence makes him nervous, so much the better. Get that case of nerves over during rehearsals. There will be enough new ones on opening night!

An audience of adults, even one or two, relieves the boredom of practice. I do stress that the audience should be parents. I never allow a child's friends to attend rehearsal. Peer pressure produces giggles and silliness and a serious rehearsal is almost impossible. I have allowed a child's *younger* brother or sister to watch but *never* an older sibling. Younger children may feel self-conscious about acting before an older child. Perhaps they are afraid the older child will criticize their acting or singing ability or will tease the young actor about the size of her part, etc. It just seems to solve all kinds of problems to restrict attendance at rehearsals.

One way to keep rehearsal interesting is to introduce props. The term "props" is a nickname for properties, those items used on stage other than scenery. Children think it's fun to carry baskets, suitcases, books and other items on stage and it gives them something to do with their hands. Learning to handle props introduces a new element to rehearsal. In *Oklahoma!* the girls gathering at Laurey's house carried picnic baskets to be auctioned off later at the Skidmore party. At one point they had to put down the baskets, and six girls had to pick up and open umbrellas to be used in the dance that followed. This doesn't magically happen. It must be rehearsed.

Then there was the time when Curly sold his saddle to gain more money with which to bid for Laurey's picnic basket. We'd found a pony saddle for our young cowboy, and the first time he used it he dragged it across the stage as though it weighed five hundred pounds. I showed him how to grab the pommel and swing the saddle across his shoulder to hang down his back. It took a little practice, but soon he handled the saddle like a real cowboy.

Another way to break the monotony of February is to add the musical numbers to the scenes. During January it is better to leave the songs out. Children need to practice those numbers and they do not want to sing even for other cast members until they feel confident. During January soloists practice the songs with the musical director or accompanist only. When our school music teacher fills this job, she works with the soloists in music class, just as she teaches the entire group the songs sung by everyone on stage. This even includes the stage crew, prompter, and those who have chosen to paint scenery only. Everyone learns all the songs. This is another way of drawing the group together, of learning to work as a team.

At the time the show is cast I ask all soloists to purchase a tape or compact disc of the Broadway show music and to listen to the songs they will sing in our show. My reasoning is that the song was done by professionals, and who better for a child to learn from than a professional? The soloists work with their songs as well as their lines in the privacy of their own homes. By the time January rehearsals roll around, the children have a good grasp of the music. I suppose we could use the music in rehearsals before February, but I simply choose not to. It gives our February rehearsals a boost, just when we need it. The first time a child sings in full rehearsal, the cast breaks into applause. What a proud moment for that young soloist! Recognition from one's peers is the sweetest nectar in the world.

At the beginning of March we move rehearsal to the music room/stage, which gives those days the "sparkle" we need. It is exciting to work on a real stage. As they are learning where to stand and how to use the larger stage effectively, the children realize that they do not yet know all there is about this play. They are again interested in learning.

By this time all the children have bonded into a true team. They can laugh at each other's mistakes, and no one takes offense or makes fun of another. One day our leading man was absent from school because of illness, and we had to work around him in rehearsals. I climbed on stage, script in hand, and read his lines in the appropriate places, exaggerating the expression in my voice. The children thought it was hilarious. They loved it! When we came to a place where he was to sing a song, the children knew I could not sing, and they were wondering what I was going to do. Well, I mouthed the words while the musical director sang offstage. It surely added spice to that rehearsal! We did not accomplish much that day, but the time was not wasted because the attitude of the children received such a boost.

I also remember a time when we were rehearsing *Annie Get Your Gun*. Most girls wear slacks to school, but I felt Annie needed to get used to wearing a skirt and to keep her "six-shooter" in the waistband of her skirt. So, she brought a skirt from home and slipped it on over her slacks for rehearsals. Things were progressing nicely on this particular day. Annie had gestured with her gun and then stuck it in her waistband. Just as it was time for her to reach for it again, it slipped. Down it went, under her skirt and out the bottom, to land on the floor with a loud thud. She was so surprised that she simply bent over and stared at the thing lying innocently there on the stage floor in front of her. There was total silence for a minute as everyone on stage bent over and stared, too. Then the place erupted with peals of laughter! It took probably 10 minutes before *any* of us was able to calm down, director included. Rehearsal continued amid an occasional chuckle from this or that child for the rest of the afternoon. It was good for all of us.

You will find that your play generates interest in research. If the story line is fictional, your students will find out all they can about the time period in which the play takes place. For example, when we were doing *Oklahoma!* the children learned a great deal about American history during that period. This was done with absolutely no suggestion from me. They were simply interested. Once their interest left me speechless, however, as it wasn't my job to teach sex education. The story of *The King and I* is based on an actual ruler of Siam in the mid–1800s. The children were fascinated to learn that their play was based on a real man, and their research was thorough. I was quite pleased with all they were learning until one child came to me with the question, "Mrs. Ross, what's a concubine?" My reply, after I took a deep breath, was, "Why do you ask?" The child quickly explained, "It says in this book that the king had 3,000 wives and concubines." Gulp!

There seems to be one particular line in each play that is adopted by the cast as the "catch phrase" for the year. It's a line that the cast takes as its own and is very special to them, an inside joke and a symbol of their working together on such an important project. It is never planned; it just happens. The line is used over and over again in all kinds of everyday situations and always makes the children laugh. When our show was *The Music Man*, in 1980, we had a tiny girl cast as Winthrop. This child had a voice to match her size. When she said the line, "Do I hafta?" the entire cast broke up in laughter. From then on, that was the by-word for that show. It was used in rehearsals and also in the regular classroom, whenever something arose that didn't exactly suit someone. "Do I hafta?" It *always* inspired laughter from the children, and also from the director!

Near the end of March a letter goes home to the parents detailing dates and times of dress rehearsals and performances and when the children should report for makeup, even though this information is already contained on the rehearsal schedule that each parent already has. Permission slips needed for the rest of the activities connected with the show are attached. This is an example of the letter.

Dear Parents,
   The great moment is drawing near! Here is a final schedule of show dates and times. Please keep this and refer to it during the next few weeks. Also, please fill in and return to school the attached permission slip. The children may not participate unless we have them.

   April 1—All costumes are to be brought to school—ON HANGERS! Shoes and accessories should be in a bag attached to the hanger.
   April 3 (Friday)—Dress Rehearsal at Cedar Park School.
   1:00 P.M.—Children change into their costumes and report to the makeup table to have their makeup applied by parents on the makeup committee.

2:00 P.M.—Dress Rehearsal. Pictures will be taken by the cast photographer.

April 6 (Monday)—Dress Rehearsal.

1:00 P.M.—Children get into costumes and have their makeup applied by makeup committee .

2:00 P.M.—Dress Rehearsal

April 7 (Tuesday)—School performance!

8:00 A.M.—Children arrive at school and get into their costumes; have makeup applied by makeup committee.

9:15 A.M.—Performance for students of Cedar Park School. *(Note: Sometimes students from another school will attend this performance.)*

CHILDREN TAKE THEIR COSTUMES HOME WITH THEM THIS AFTERNOON BECAUSE FOR THE NEXT PERFORMANCES THEY WILL DRESS AT HOME AND ARRIVE AT SCHOOL FOR MAKEUP ONLY.

April 8 (Wednesday)—NO REHEARSAL

April 9 (Thursday)—Community Performance.

6:30 P.M.—Children arrive at school—IN COSTUME—and committee applies makeup.

7:30 P.M.—Performance!

April 10 (Friday)—Community Performance

6:30 P.M.—Children arrive at school—IN COSTUME—and committee applies makeup.

7:30 P.M.—Performance!

9:00 P.M.—Cast party in the school cafeteria for cast members and their families.

This ends over three months of work for a wonderful cast of children. I hope they never forget the experience they have had. It has been a pleasure to work with them!

Sincerely,
Beverly Ross

---

*PLEASE FILL OUT THIS PERMISSION
SLIP AND RETURN IT TO SCHOOL.*

My child, _____, has permission to participate in the performances of *The Wizard of Oz* on the evenings of April 9–10.

Signed_____

Dress Rehearsal

And so passes March. From here on, excitement is high. Scenery is added during the last week of regular rehearsals so the stage crew can get used to handling it without mishaps. Children bring their costumes to school on hangers. You have practiced the full play daily for

A child's reaction to the exuberant applause from the audience.

the past four days and are ready for Dress Rehearsal. Actually, the only change in routine is the addition of costumes and makeup. Two classrooms are designated as dressing rooms, one for the boys and one for the girls. If there is a window in the classroom door, it is covered with black construction paper to insure privacy for those changing clothes. Any costumes that will be worn in later scenes must be carried to the backstage area. Find places to hang the costume *changes* backstage so that each child knows where to look for his or hers.

The children must practice getting in and out of their costumes in the allotted time. For an Indian dance in one of our shows, the children slipped their Indian costumes *over* their other costumes. At the first dress rehearsal we waited and waited for the dancers to make their entrance. Finally, frustrated, I called, "What's holding things up? Come out—now!" Well, they did, though one poor child was still carrying his costume pants in his hand! Two dress rehearsals are necessary to work out new problems that arise.

In early April when we are finally ready to perform for an audience, we put on our show for the students in our school. They make an excellent first audience. They are not critical of the efforts of these

Excellent costume choices by the parents of Annie and Miss Hannigan in *Annie*.

talented and well-polished young actors. It also gives the children a chance to become accustomed to a large audience before they perform for the entire community.

Their first performance produces results that will bring tears of joy to your eyes. You are so proud of them! They did it! After you recover, your "director nerves" will set in. You have spent three months trying to produce the best possible show. Have you succeeded? Our community audience is judge and jury for us. You know they will like it, but that's not good enough. You want to knock their eyeballs out!

6

Directing

Directions to the cast will mean the difference between a mediocre kids' show and a dynamite professional quality show whose actors just happen to be kids. The key to success is the director's attention to detail. Even the smallest gesture, a smile or a nod, in the right place adds to the overall effect. Children won't think of these things at first; the director must. So let's get started! Today is the first rehearsal. The children have awaited this moment for three months, and they are filled with excitement. You have chosen your rehearsal area and have marked off the stage according to your needs. Tell the children which portion of the stage they are to use for exits and entrances, such as the back two corners. Impress on everyone, especially those who are offstage waiting to enter, that absolute quiet is necessary backstage. If you set strict behavioral rules on the first day and stick to them, life will be much easier during the next few months.

Blocking Out the Action

On the first day and each day during the next three weeks, your major emphasis will be on "blocking out" the action of the play. This includes such things as where to stand when certain lines are said, the timing for entrances and exits and grouping when there are more than a few people on stage. For some reason, when eight or ten children are on stage, they always stand in a semicircle, all watching the person talking in the center of the stage. This looks like a chorus line to the audience, and you must continually remind the children to assemble in small groups instead. I used a hand signal, spreading apart the fingers on each of my hands, and then curling my fingers. This meant "get into group" or simply "bunch up." This was effective, even in the middle of a performance.

In a group scene, where nonspeaking actors are standing in groups at the back of the stage while speaking action takes place at the front, it looks artificial if those in the back simply stand in their groups. I tell them to pretend they are talking to each other, using various facial expressions and occasional hand gestures, but *never* are they to utter a sound! To have children talking, even quietly, at the back of the stage draws the audience's attention away from those speaking, and therefore part of the story—whatever the actors are saying—is lost. So, the nonspeakers simply make their mouths move *silently*, give an occasional hand gesture and look from one to another as though speaking to the entire group. It's effective when viewed from the audience.

"Slow and Loud"

From the first day of rehearsals to the last, I always insist that the children speak in loud voices. They must become accustomed to this method of speaking, and so they are required to do it with every single word spoken. A nervous child who is performing in front of an audience will automatically speak at a faster rate and in a softer tone than normal. Thus, the reverse must become second nature to him, and the only way to achieve that is to practice it every single day.

The rate of speaking is as important as the volume. A child must be taught to speak so slowly that when he is nervous in a performance and speaks at a more rapid pace, he is still able to be understood by the audience. I require my children to speak so slowly at first that they feel quite foolish. It becomes a joke to them. I demand to hear not only every word but also every syllable. I stand at the back of the room and insist that they adjust their volume and rate of speech so that I can hear and understand them. I remind them that they will someday be performing in a much larger room than our rehearsal area. "Slow and Loud"—those are my by-words!

These two keys—volume and rate—receive more frequent comment from our audiences than any other feature of our plays. Adults simply cannot believe that young children are capable of speech delivery that is so easily understood even far back in the audience. At this point in rehearsals I make no allowances for possible future use of microphones. The voices of young children are pitched higher than older children, and this makes them more difficult to understand if they do not compensate for it. With training in volume and rate, beginning with the first day of rehearsal and continuing all the way through with no relaxation of demand, children are able to create a play in which every single line is understood. I have sometimes wished that professional actors took as much care to be understood as do my children!

Eye Contact

Your next rule for children on stage should be: "Face front at all times. Never turn your body farther toward the side of the stage than the corners of the room facing you." Perhaps a professional actor can get away with turning her back to an audience, but a child? NEVER! Her voice simply will not carry if she turns too far around. I have a 4 × 4-inch card with a frowning face drawn on it that I insert into the back pocket or belt of a child who habitually turns too far around. When I am able to see the face on the card, the child has positioned herself incorrectly. The child feels rather foolish with this card in her back pocket and is conscious of keeping it hidden from me by turning her face and body toward the front of the stage.

Another important point to stress is that the child should look at the person to whom she is speaking! This seems like a logical thing to do, and it should not have to be taught. Yet, once a child has memorized her lines, she is inclined to simply stand on stage and recite them. To me this says "Kids' Play," and I am not satisfied with producing a kids' play. I want the children to use professional techniques. So I continually stress to each child that she must look at the person to whom she is talking. The reverse is also true. If someone on stage is talking to her, she must look at that person. To do otherwise would be impolite in society, and you are trying to create realism. Some children, as well as some adults, have trouble making eye contact with another individual. Those children must be directed to give the *illusion* of looking right at the other person. Perhaps they can look at the other person's nose or hairline. The audience will believe that the child is looking into the other's eyes.

Directing for Success

Another hint: a child expecting to enter on a particular cue line will usually wait until the other child has finished speaking that line

In *Annie Get Your Gun,* Frank Butler tells Annie Oakley she's not enough woman for him.

before he enters. This creates "dead" time while the audience waits for the child to walk across the stage to speak. Your entrance cues should be words *in* a sentence rather than at the end of a sentence. Thus, the child has entered and gone to his proper place before it is his turn to speak. He could begin speaking as he approaches the others. This method looks the most natural. You must point out these things to children. In their daily lives they walk and talk at the same time. Yet on stage they won't do this unless directed to do so.

At most rehearsals you will have no audience or perhaps only a parent or two in February and March. Children must be taught to allow time for audience reaction, even before there is an audience. Point out that they should not say the next line while the audience is still laughing about a previous one. Yet they must not wait until *all* laughter stops. The pause is determined by the amount and volume of audience laughter. The children must develop their own sense of timing in this. I encourage any parent who is watching a rehearsal to respond to script lines in order to help the children perfect their timing. We always applaud at the end of a song to help the children in those situations, too.

As children rehearse and learn the lines of other characters as well as their own, they tend to "mouth" the words as others say them aloud. Most do not realize that they do this and will deny it if you point it out. They must make a conscious effort not to be guilty of this, for it is *very* distracting to an audience. It just isn't "professional." I remember one child who chronically had this problem. We finally solved it by having him place his tongue lightly behind his upper teeth to remind him to keep his lips still. He was so busy remembering what to do with his tongue that he completely forgot his "mouthing the words" habit.

Sometimes in rehearsing a script you will find a word or phrase that a particular child has difficulty saying clearly. I recall a line from one play that gave us trouble. Our ten-year-old leading man simply could not say "jewelry" so that it was clear to an audience. So "jewelry" was changed to "sparkle," and the problem was solved. Without my insistence that I be able to understand every word spoken, I might have overlooked that tiny problem. Remember, *no* problem is tiny enough to be allowed to slip by. A solution is always waiting to be found.

Be aware of hand gestures. Even children who use their hands all the time tend to stand stiffly on stage. They must be told, particularly during early rehearsals, exactly what hand gestures to use and when. Later when they are more relaxed and "feel" their parts to a greater degree, they will include hand gestures without prompting from you. If you do not let them know in the early stages that hand gestures are okay, even preferred, they may not develop others on their own later. Be sure to instruct the children to use their "backstage" hands when gesturing. That is the hand nearest the back of the stage. In using a "front-stage" hand, a child may turn his body too far around toward the back and thus may not be heard distinctly. Also, gesturing with a front-stage hand draws the audience's eye to the hand rather than to the actor's face. This will not happen if the backstage hand is used.

While we are on the subject of gesturing, you or your musical director should instruct the children to use hand motions in songs. A child standing frozen on stage, singing a song, looks most uncomfortable, and usually is. If a song mentions "sun," have the child make a motion toward the sky; a galloping horse could be indicated by holding invisible reins and moving them up and down slightly. Flowers could be indicated by sweeping the hand toward the ground. If you have difficulty thinking of gestures, go over the song line by line with the music director and child, and absorb what the lyrics are trying to say. Then ideas will come to you easily. The child will also make suggestions, which you should agree with and praise. Also be sure to tell the children it is okay to move around while singing. Two or three steps in one direction or another and back again looks quite natural.

So much can be done with the eyes! Adults who know how to make their eyes "sparkle" add much to their personality. So it is with children, particularly on stage. This is a skill that must be learned and consciously practiced, preferably in front of a mirror. Once mastered it may be used whether on- or offstage, with excellent results in dealing with others. If a teenager uses it, it's a powerful flirting technique. Open your eyes wide, consciously try to make them bright, and perhaps dart them quickly from place to place. This gives a shiny glow over your entire face. Such sparkle from an actor onstage is very distinctive. The audience becomes caught up in the character's personality. It is particularly charming when it comes from a child actor. Teach this skill to your children and hope they use it offstage as well as onstage. It even helps to create an optimistic mental attitude and makes one a person whose company others enjoy.

Psychology plays an important part in producing a successful play with children. The feelings and ego of the child must be constantly considered. After the first couple of weeks of rehearsals some children will stand out as being exceptionally good in their parts. Their peers recognize this, also. Those children continue to need encouragement, of course, but not as much as the children who are still weak in their characterizations. If an ego begins to drag, the performance suffers. So praise while correcting those children, and remember to do it in front of the cast. This is contagious, and they will begin to compliment each other. Everyone benefits.

The Love Scene

The love scene in your play deserves special mention because it is a psychologically trying time for the youngsters involved. My cardinal rule is that no child is allowed to laugh at the participants in that scene. I warn everyone that the first penalty for laughing is the culprit will be made to play the scene himself. The penalty for a second offense is to be sent home from rehearsals. This is a disgrace in front of all the others. I have never had to use either punishment. Just knowing what will happen is enough to deter laughing!

Dorothy's and Scarecrow's faces light up the stage in *The Wizard of Oz*.

Naturally, the love scene does not ever involve a kiss. The most that can be expected from children this age is hand-holding. You can do much with this simple gesture to get the idea across to an audience. There is usually a love song involved. My two participants stand alone at center stage. One is singing to the other and looking directly into the eyes of that person. Toward the end of the song the boy takes the girl's backstage hand. Then he takes her other hand during the last line of the song. The effect on the audience as they watch these youngsters is electric. They get the message! If there is no song involved in that part of the scene, the same hand-holding sequence can be performed while the lines are spoken. The eye contact is essential here. Make sure your lead characters are able to look directly into the eyes of another person while talking.

If one of your participants in the love scene has difficulty speaking a line, tell her to imagine that she is talking not to a classmate but to an adult. She can imagine that she is reciting to her teacher, parent or relative. This suggestion has worked for me. I must confess though that one of our leading ladies simply could not speak a particular line because she was too embarrassed. I considered that line

The love interest is gently portrayed by hand-holding and eye contact.

essential to the scene, and I was unwilling to change it. The poor child giggled, turned red in the face, and couldn't even look at her leading man when she said the line. We all dreaded that point in rehearsals because she began to act so silly. By calling her at home after rehearsing that scene, I began to build her confidence. I told her that if she continued in that behavior she would affect the performance of her leading man, as well as draw even more attention to herself and her uncomfortable position. If she treated the situation as normal and spoke that line as though it did not bother her, her peers would accept it as part of the play. I finally convinced her that if she were able to do that line as I instructed, others would simply view it as another part of the script rather than a particularly difficult line.

This advice applies to any child who is secretly embarrassed to recite certain lines. The shy child may feel this way just by having to speak on stage. This feeling in no way diminishes his desire to have a speaking part. Treating his lines as perfectly normal makes his peers accept them in the same way. Children soon begin to accept all lines in a play as coming from the characters in the story rather than from classmates. You can help this along by a simple trick. Never call the children by their given names in rehearsals. *Always* use their stage names when addressing them. This helps them think of one another as the characters in the play rather than as classmates. Audiences accept them in the same way. A frequent comment about our plays from audiences is, "After about ten minutes you forget the actors are children." The self-confidence gained by all the children is incredible. They have accomplished something they never thought possible—performing for many people. Even the child who is normally outgoing and confident feels that she has accomplished something truly remarkable. And she has!

Technical Help

Technical aids are extremely helpful in rehearsals. I always record every rehearsal. Afterwards I listen to the tape and make notes on problems I detect. My tape recorder has a counter that enables me to note the exact place on the tape where something is not right. The next day I go over all my notes with the children, and I am able to play problem portions of the tape for them. Telling a child that he spoke too softly or too rapidly is not nearly as effective as letting him hear himself on a tape. Children are embarrassed to hear themselves on tape, especially during early rehearsals and especially when the rest of the cast is listening. This feeling lessens as more and more tapes are played in the following days and weeks. The tape fills another need as well. It is useful in demonstrating to the child or to the class what a fine job a certain person did in rehearsal. Whether shy or confident, the child reacts to public praise with even greater effort at the next rehearsal.

As director you gain much from listening to the tapes. You find lines that have a slightly different emphasis than you would like, and you are able to talk to the child involved so that she can change them. You may *think* that you absorb everything during a rehearsal, but there is so much going on that in truth you miss a great deal. The tape gives you another chance to find errors, and in correcting them you create a more polished show. After you and the children listen to the tape, re-record on that same tape during the next rehearsal. This is an inexpensive though beneficial aid to all concerned.

Creative Problem Solving

As the weeks of rehearsal pass, you will find that the children, even the main characters, have memorized their lines at the beginning of the script much more thoroughly than those toward the middle and the end. The child who is struggling to remember lines cannot also keep in mind your many stage directions. It is usually necessary at some point in rehearsals for me to show my displeasure at those who forget lines. Once I "make a scene" the children usually go back to studying their scripts. I tell them that no matter how well they think they know their parts, it is essential for them to study each night for the next day's rehearsal. I am not sure they do it—certainly not all of them do—but it makes *me* feel better! One can always hope that at least some do take the advice.

Sometimes when a problem arises you simply cannot solve it no matter how hard you try. If this happens, ask a friend to attend rehearsal and give you impressions or suggestions. The year we were producing *Annie Get Your Gun* we had what I began to think was an unsolvable problem. In the story there is a shooting contest between Annie Oakley and Frank Butler. The children wore toy guns and holsters, which they would use in this contest. The question was how to make the guns look and sound as if they were being fired at real targets. We tried every system of sound effects that we thought safe and appropriate for use with children. We scoured theatrical supply houses, library books and any other source that occurred to us. I finally decided that whatever we used would simply have to look and sound artificial. A child offstage slapped two small boards together while Annie and Frank fired stage right and imitated the recoil of their guns. Sometimes they were able to time their recoil gesture with the sound of the gun, but sometimes they missed by just enough to make it noticeable to the audience. A better solution did not seem possible, though. Then one day our stage manager, Anne, came up with a suggestion that we change the way the children stood, giving the audience a front view of them instead of a side view. From that angle the recoil seemed to match the gunshot sound every time and everything looked perfectly natural! Such a simple solution! Sometimes "new eyes" can solve a problem that has seemed insurmountable. (See chapter 11 under *Sound Effects* for a full description of this problem as well as how to handle other sound effects.)

As you produce your play you will encounter unique difficulties that I have not. You will solve them the best way you can. Keep in mind that with experience comes expertise. With your first theatrical efforts, your audience will be anticipating something that looks typical of what they expect from children. They will be amazed at what you and the children have created! They will rave! Then as the years and the plays go by, your audience will expect more because they know what has been accomplished in the past. You will be ready for the challenge. They expect more and your experience enables you to produce a more polished show each year. Soon you and your children will be a true phenomenon, exceeding the expectations of even the most critical audience. The children, hearing the applause and the glowing compliments after the show, will feel that they have accomplished something beyond their wildest dreams! The feelings of self-worth and self-confidence developed in all of the children are feelings that every human being ought to be able to experience, but many never do. If you ever needed a reward for all your hard work, this is it!

7

Music

Music is the beauty and the backbone of your show. If it is well done, your audience will leave the theater humming. Although you can learn from this book most of the skills you will need to produce a Broadway show with your students, music is not one of them. Unless you are a musician yourself, you will need help with musical accompaniment and voice coaching.

The musical accompanist's job is just what the title suggests—playing the piano for the children as they sing. Although many adults can play the piano skillfully, not all of them will be able to fulfill the demands of this critically important position.

The musical accompanist must understand the importance of *playing softly.* Children's singing voices are not loud by nature. The children work hard during three months of rehearsals to obtain more volume. To be overshadowed by the piano is dreadful! Not only will the child feel cheated, but so will the audience, who did not come to the show to hear someone play the piano. They came to hear the children sing. Have you ever been to a professional theatrical performance where the orchestra obscured the lyrics being sung by the actors? It happens more often than you would expect. Do not allow this to happen in your show. From the very beginning of musical rehearsal, make sure your accompanist is aware of the singers' volume and adjusts the instrument's volume accordingly.

The musical accompanist must be willing and able to give a lot of time to the play. He or she must be present during every rehearsal beginning in February at the very least. January would be even better. If the musical accompanist cannot attend the earliest rehearsals, it is possible to use a tape recording of the songs made by the accompanist. You may find that this is sometimes an unsatisfactory arrangement. Dealing with the tape recorder and finding the right song on that long tape in the midst of rehearsal can be cumbersome and time consuming. Personally, I'd rather have the child sing without the music than to have to bother with a tape recorder.

If you are lucky enough to find one, the voice coach is a jewel! This person's job is to work with the soloists to perfect their singing, diction and volume. The coach's work will begin in January when drama rehearsals begin but will have to be scheduled either before school, after rehearsals or on weekends. As children master their songs, voice coaching sessions are gradually phased out.

Children can be taught to increase their singing volume, and some methods for doing so are described later in this chapter. If you cannot recruit a voice coach and the accompanist cannot perform this job, it is best to choose children who have natural singing volume in audition. The child-soloists will have to learn all of their songs through imitation. Each child purchases an audio tape or a compact disc of the Broadway show. The singers on the recording are professionals, and the children can learn much from listening to them and imitating what they hear. Later, when the accompanist joins rehearsals, the child learns to sing the songs with the piano music.

Musical Director

If the music teacher at your school is willing to accept the job of musical director, the show music might be woven into the daily curriculum. The music teacher has the advantage of knowing the students and is accustomed to accompanying them on the piano.

However, many music teachers serve several schools and it may not be possible for her or him to attend after-school rehearsals. If that is the case, you must recruit a parent or other volunteer from the school community. As soon as you have chosen your script, begin searching for this talented and dedicated gem. Start with the parents of your cast members. Parents are more likely to be willing to give the necessary time than someone who has no child in the show. Don't overlook teenage brothers and sisters who may have extraordinary talent and years of piano lessons behind them.

If you are unable to recruit a musical accompanist from your parent pool, put a notice in your school's PTA newsletter, explaining that you plan to put on a Broadway musical with your students and that you need an accompanist to participate in rehearsals and performances daily over at least a two-month period. If you have no luck there, expand your search to include nearby schools, churches and other community groups. A senior citizen would be perfect! He or she would be retired from the working world and therefore free to attend all rehearsals and performances. I can't tell you how many times I have wished I played the piano!

When recruiting for an accompanist and/or voice coach, I am careful not to mention the formal title of "Musical Director" because it can be intimidating. We bestow the title later, after we've completed rehearsals and the volunteer's confidence is as high as that of our young actors. Adults respond to and need recognition and praise too.

Tips for the Accompanist

Every show needs an overture. It signals the beginning and quiets the audience for the performance to begin. The overture is composed of part of most songs in the show. If you are not using all the songs written for the original show, you may not wish to use the original overture. Your accompanist must arrange a condensed overture.

Choose the most important, best-known song in the show for the opening and closing sections of the overture. For example, in the show *Annie* the song "Tomorrow" would come first and last. In between these, place the choruses of other songs. Note in what keys they are written and never place two songs side by side if they are written in the same key. The overture is uninteresting if all the music is in the same key. In addition to the key, look at the tempo of the songs. Do not group all fast songs and all slow songs together. Alternate a fast one with a slow one. If you do not wish to use the entire chorus of each song, choose only the parts you prefer. You will need at least four to eight measures of each, however. Examine the notes at the end of one song and choose the next, in a different key and tempo, that will be easy to slide into. You are simply modulating your keys as you go through the overture.

For the evening performance you will have about a five-minute overture. Begin three minutes before show time so that any of the audience not yet in their seats have time to be seated. Then the overture extends two minutes into show time, so that everyone becomes quiet and ready for the show to begin. The house lights dim, the curtain opens and the children are on their own!

When we took our show to other schools, our overture began as the last few groups of students filed in to take their seats. The music quiets the audience, and the show can begin on time. This situation may require a longer overture. You may repeat the entire musical arrangement or you may prepare an entirely different overture that lasts longer. Your main object is to quiet the audience and set the mood for the show. Then it's curtain time!

Voice Coach

You may be extremely lucky to find among your parents or within the community an experienced voice coach who is willing to work on your show. This marvelous person turned up in the parent pool of our first show in the person of Sandy, whose son was in the show. A voice major in college, Sandy was our combination voice coach-musical accompanist for six years, and she was a marvel. I did my best during that time to absorb most of her tricks for getting singing volume from the children. In later years, when Sandy was no longer working with us, I was able to describe those methods to the soloists. I had to leave it strictly up to them as to whether or not they practiced these things on their own, as I certainly didn't have time to drill them. Perhaps at least some of them took advantage of this knowledge. One can only hope. In any case, Sandy's methods are described in this chapter for your voice coach in hopes they will help your children produce better music in their show.

Tips for the Voice Coach

The play is cast, the winter holiday is over, drama and voice rehearsals begin in January. Consider holding voice rehearsals for soloists before school each morning because the children will attend drama rehearsals after school. Arrange a rehearsal schedule with the soloists' parents. Find a practice area in your school where there is a piano and privacy. Meet with the male and female leads twice a week at first and always on the same days of the week so the children remember to come. Meet with the secondary leads once a week.

Lesson 1: Getting Acquainted

Never use the child's given name during a voice rehearsal. Always call him by his show name, just as the director does in regular drama

Annie and Warbucks are "Together at Last" in *Annie*.

rehearsals. This helps him to realize that when he steps onto the stage, he ceases to be himself and becomes his play character. Even in Hollywood, actors refer to the characters they are playing as "he" or "she," rather than "I" or "me." By the time you begin working on the love song, you will have already established this difference, and you can approach the children with, "Don't be embarrassed to hold her hand. It is not you, the fifth-grade child, doing it. It is you, the character in the play."

At the first voice rehearsal, the child will want to start singing, "right now." It is best to get acquainted first. Although the child knows his teacher-director well, you are someone new who will be telling him what to do in the coming weeks. You do not know each other, and it's hard to trust a stranger. Begin by telling a little of your musical background so that the child will have faith in your knowledge and the things you will teach. Ask the child about other activities and interests he or she may have. You must help the child find times to practice at home. If he is terribly busy with another activity this month but expects things to settle down next month, you need to know about it. Be reasonable in your demands. The child will appreciate it and will work harder for you.

Next comes a brief anatomy lesson. The child-singer needs to know something about sound production in the human body. Explain how the vocal cords work. Use rubber bands to demonstrate. A thin band represents the vocal cords when singing high notes, a medium band for medium notes and a heavy band for low notes. The vocal cords vibrate when a person sings, producing the sound. If you pluck each band in turn, the different tones can be heard.

Tell the child about the vocal selections book and its cost. The children playing the leads need this book. Available at any good music store, it contains the songs for the play. All soloists must have their own copy since you will be making notations on each soloist's music for his or her use only. Suggest that the child purchase the compact disc or tape of the Broadway show. Listening to professionals will help the child learn the melodies and lyrics of the songs. He or she must learn the songs *before* beginning to use the vocal selections book. Does this seem backwards to you? It really is not. The sheet music is not for memorizing purposes. It is for work on diction and breathing. If the child had the vocal selections book, a parent might, with the best of intentions, be tempted to play the songs on a piano at home and teach them to the child incorrectly. It is easier for the child to learn a song correctly from the vocal coach in the first place than to have to unlearn one thing and then learn something else.

Tell the child you will be making a voice lesson on tape for her to use in practice sessions at home. Explain that the child needs to find a time at home, when she is *alone*, to practice away from teasing brothers and sisters. If the house is always busy, perhaps the child could find a quiet corner of the yard or take a walk and practice while walking. The reason for this seclusion is that no one, and particularly a child, wants to do poorly when performing in front of others. The child who begins to practice new songs may have difficulty at first.

That is why privacy is necessary. The only exception is when the child is working with you, the voice coach. There it is perfectly all right to sound "bad." If she sounded great from the beginning, she would not need you. You are there to help the child learn to sound great, so that when others hear her perform, they will be impressed!

To conclude Lesson one, sing one song from the show for the child. Discuss what the song is trying to say, the purpose for it and the type of attitude with which it should be performed by the character. For example, an exciting song would fall dead if not sung with animation. A cowboy would sing a song in a different style than would a king.

Lesson 2: Diction and Breathing

Back to anatomy: this time explain what a diaphragm is and how it works. Paint a visual picture for the child in describing the diaphragm in relation to the lungs. Tell him to imagine a zipper on the front of his chest. Unzip the zipper and put a blown-up balloon representing the lungs inside; then close the zipper. The diaphragm is the muscle right underneath that balloon. The balloon, when filled with air, pushes the muscle down lower in the body. When the balloon deflates, the muscle raises up to push out the air. This muscle, the diaphragm, is very important in singing because it helps control our breathing. Singers should develop this muscle so that they can let the air out of their lungs slowly and evenly, rather than all at once.

A good way for the child to develop this muscle is to lie flat on his back on a bed with knees bent and feet flat on the bed. The child places a book on the diaphragm, located right underneath the rib cage. Then without moving the shoulders at all, the child raises and then lowers the book. Doing this exercise every night before he goes to sleep will strengthen the diaphragm muscle and help the child to sing better and with more volume. This exercise should be done while lying down each day for the first month of work. Then encourage the child to try it while standing up, using his hands instead of a book and raising and lowering them by using the diaphragm muscle.

During Lesson two, begin work on a song. Together you will go through one song in the child's vocal selections book, marking all of the music for two purposes: diction and breathing. Place a check mark in every spot where the child should take a breath. She is always required to breathe at that point, even if she feels she can sing longer without a breath. A nervous child on stage will need more oxygen than one in rehearsal, and breathing points should be more frequent than seem necessary at first.

The diction markings stress certain *consonants* in words. A child of this age should stress *l, m, n, t,* and *d*. She must be *sure* to pronounce these consonants, particularly when they fall at the beginning or the end of a word. The only stressed *vowel* sound for a child this young should be the long vowel sound. So in marking the music underline each place where one of the stress consonants appears *at the beginning or end of a word*. Also, underline all long vowel sounds. Use a red pen so that these points will stand out.

Sometimes, even when a child stresses the proper letters, a word may be difficult to understand when sung. Perhaps that word and the next one sound as if they run together, particularly if the first word ends with the letter *l* or *n*. In that case, for diction purposes insert the word "a" in between. For example, to sharpen the sound of "you will stand," have the child sing "you will a stand." Your young singer will think, "That sounds dumb!" Assure her that from the audience "a" will not be heard, because as she becomes accustomed to saying it, she will slide over it, not stressing its pronunciation.

Only one song is studied and marked at each session with the child. That adds emphasis to it and helps her understanding. To cover all of the songs that a lead character must sing will take several sessions, but by meeting with the child twice a week, you will soon cover all of them. Once a song has been marked, the child may work on it alone at home. No parent help yet, please!

After the music is marked, you will sing a phrase of the song, and then the child will sing it with you. The child will then sing it alone while you listen. Work out the first phrase in this way, then the second phrase, and then put the two together. Proceed through the entire song in this manner.

Explain to the child the importance of opening the mouth while singing. No matter how much lung power she has, she will produce no volume if the sound can't get out! By holding the first two fingers of her hand together and placing them between the upper and lower front teeth, the child will find that this is the best position for achieving the most volume. Of course, some words require that the mouth be closed for pronunciation. You cannot sing the word "need" with an open mouth, but use this skill whenever possible.

A skill that must always be practiced is *breathing evenly*. Instruct the child to wet her fingers and hold them in front of her mouth. Then she is to take a deep breath and let the air out *evenly*. The dampness will enable her to feel the air flow over her fingers. Another excellent exercise to encourage even breathing is done with a lighted candle. For the children's safety, mention this technique to the *parents only*. Most parents are willing to supervise such an activity at home. The lighted candle trick is done by placing a candle in a sturdy holder and lighting it. The singer places herself in front of the candle, fills her lungs with air and exhales. The object is to exhale slowly enough so that the candle flame merely flickers but does not go out. Keep the flame moving until the lungs are out of air. This teaches excellent breath control, but it must be practiced under adult supervision.

Lesson 3: Volume and Range

At the beginning of this lesson, explain the necessity for warm-ups. Draw a parallel to athletes who always limber up their muscles before practice or a game to prevent injury. The same is true of singers. You have only one set of vocal cords. Take good care of them!

Warm-ups (or vocalizing) consist of singing five notes in succession with the piano and using the words "lah," "lay," or "lee" in turn. Sing "lah-lah-lah-lah-lah" up the scale and then back down. Then the child begins a half note higher and goes through the same process again, up five notes and then down five notes. Continue this procedure until the child has gone as high as he can sing. Next he begins at the top note and sings down the scale for five notes and then back up to the starting note. Then he begins a half step lower and does the same thing—down and up. He continues until he has sung as low as he can. Keep track on a chart of the date and the note range (the highest and the lowest notes sung). As his singing range increases day by day, the child will be amazed that he is singing higher and lower than ever before. Here are the results in black and white. He begins to see that you really know what you are doing. This will reinforce his trust in your advice and he will be willing to try whatever you suggest from now on.

During warm-ups pull out your mirror and ask the child to watch his mouth in it. He must always open his mouth wide enough when singing "lah" to insert those two fingers between his teeth. When singing "lee," he must always produce a smile. From now on, a mirror is an essential part of his equipment, as important as his music. Whenever he is practicing at home, he must sing in front of a mirror —either one in his bedroom or a small one if he is out walking. With this one lesson you are teaching techniques for obtaining volume and range in singing. Vocalizing must precede every rehearsal and performance from now on. This is very important!

Never allow the child to sit during a voice rehearsal. Posture is extremely important in singing. The child must stand straight, shoulders back. In these early rehearsals, his hands must be clasped behind his back. When practicing at home after a long day at school, if the child is tired and feels he must sit for practice, tell him to sit on the edge of a chair, his back not touching the chair, his shoulders back and hands clasped behind him.

One of the best tricks for increasing volume is a method by which you have the child focus his tone in singing. Draw a large "X" on a chart, and place it as far from the child as possible in the room where you are working. Have him focus on that "X" and sing directly to it. Every word of every song must "hit" the center of that "X." You may not hear the results of this exercise for weeks. If you tape-record a child's singing during one of the first lessons and then make another tape several weeks later, the improvement will be quite evident. The volume of the child's singing voice will be greatly increased. The "X" represents the audience although the child does not realize it.

There was one child who developed excellent singing volume through the use of these techniques. In the beginning she always seemed to lose volume during a song. When that occurred, she was told to omit the words of the song and just sing "lah" for a phrase or two and then go back to the words. By the time our performances were held, she was able to sustain the volume through her entire song. This was a big hurdle for her, and she felt very proud of her accomplishment! So did we!

For this and subsequent lessons, continue to mark the music of one song per day until you have covered all of them. Review the songs previously marked, which the child has been practicing at home.

Voice Lesson Tape

By the end of the first month, the child will have learned her music but must continue to practice using the techniques for diction and volume that you have taught her. The parent may now help the child at home, if there is a piano available. If the child hears the parent play something in a different way from what you have taught her, she will recognize it and be able to correct it.

February is the time for the voice lesson tape. Make up an individual tape for each child. One child's tape may contain the following. "Hi, *(character name)*. It's time for your lesson. First let's go through your warm-ups." Play the piano for the child to begin warm-ups. "Now, let's work on *(name of first song)*." Discuss briefly the problems that the child is having with this particular song and how to handle them. Play the notes the child will sing for the whole song. Then give the child the dialogue cue line that comes right before the song. After the cue, play the accompaniment, which may vary from the notes to be sung, and you sing the song. Then play the accompaniment so that the child can sing with the tape. Repeat the accompaniment so that the child may sing the song twice. Then move to the next song, listing problems and remedies, playing the notes to be sung. Go through every song that the child sings in the show in this way. The child is expected to use this tape at least three times a week at home. It is even better if she can find the time to use it daily. After the last performance of the show, ask the child to return it to you so you can use it to record a lesson for someone else next year.

The child is not left entirely to her own devices. You still meet with her twice a week. The lessons are shorter now, usually lasting 20 minutes. That means you can work with two children each morning. At this time let the child designate some of the material for the vocal lesson. By this time she knows where she is having trouble and will suggest something she feels she needs help on. Of course, you may have spotted a problem area, and you will go over that in the lesson too. In early February the child will be singing the songs in regular drama rehearsals, even though they have not yet been perfected to performance quality. The other cast members have been anxiously waiting to hear the soloists, and their applause at the end of a song gives the young singer a real ego boost. Recognition from one's peers is sweet, indeed!

Some songs require a duet, trio or quartet. Perhaps one child sings a line or two and then others sing a line. February is the time to bring those children, who have been practicing separately, together in a vocal rehearsal. Ask them to come to practice at the same time. In one of our shows, a song required four singers, each singing a different melody at the same time, similar to barbershop harmony. Children this age are usually able to handle two-part harmony, three-part once in a while with lots of work, but four-part harmony—never. So what were we to do? We used four children but only three musical parts. One child sang the top part, another sang the bottom, and the other two sang the middle part. It worked beautifully, and the audience could not detect that the harmony was three part instead of four. The quartet created a sensation in the show!

Gestures and Staging

This is a good time to work on gestures and staging for the songs. To give the child some idea of what to do with his hands, you will have to present ideas to him. Later on he may be able to think of some on his own. Without gestures he will look uncomfortable on stage. The lyrics of the songs will suggest appropriate hand gestures. For example, if the song is about musical instruments, the child might pantomime the motions of playing the instrument mentioned.

Staging a song simply means teaching the child how to move while singing. He cannot stand like a statue in one place. Just as in dramatic rehearsal, he must be taught to move around, taking a step or two in different directions or singing one line to one person and another line to someone else.

When appropriate, he should look directly at the person to whom he is singing and that person should look at him. He should remember to make his eyes sparkle, except in a sad song, which you will rarely have in a show for children. Smiling while singing *is so impor-*

In *The Music Man* the quartet practices harmonizing.

tant! Children can charm an audience as much with a smile as with a beautiful voice. Everyone loves a happy face!

The love song requires delicate handling. Your leading lady and man will be uncomfortable doing this number because of their ages. In this song, the two should sing to each other, stage center. As the next-to-last phrase is sung, the two should join backstage hands. Then during the last phrase, they join front stage hands, looking right into each other's eyes. When done correctly, these simple gestures create exactly the right mood and achieve the same effect as a kiss between adult singers at the end of such a song. The children will be inclined to drop hands and move apart as soon as they've accomplished that last hand-hold. Don't let them do it! Require that they freeze in their hand-holding position, looking into each other's eyes until the applause dies down or the lights go out, signifying the end of the scene—whichever comes first.

Musical Ups and Downs

Pitch is the single most important element you listen for in auditions. Some children simply cannot sing, and it would be cruel to force them into singing a solo. Yet I remember one little boy who stood out in auditions as being perfect for a particular part in all respects except one. His sparkling eyes and sunny personality typified the character in the play, yet Jordie was tone-deaf. He could not hit a single note that was played on the piano, much less sing a song. Unfortunately, his part called for a solo. We counted on our musical director's ability to work miracles, though we knew she would never be able to teach him to sing on pitch. The song he had to perform was very rhythmical with a strong beat. We thought he might be able to "talk" the song instead of sing it. This is difficult for children. They tend to follow precisely the rhythm of the accompaniment. Sometimes during rehearsal Jordie would begin to sing, which was disastrous! We finally taught him to talk the words in time to the music as though he were telling a story. When performance time finally arrived Jordie and his song were a huge hit! He talked, rolled those big blue eyes and carried off his number superbly.

In another show we had the same problem with another child who had a two-line solo in a number performed by a large group of children. We taught Larry to "talk" his part too. All was going well until we did the show at another school. *During* the performance we discovered that Larry's position on stage in that number placed him directly in front of a microphone. We had counted on the rest of the singers to drown him out during the rest of the song. The microphone made Larry's voice heard above all the others! Quick, a solution! We could not move Larry or the microphone so I made a sign saying "Larry—mouth the words" and held it up so he could read it from the stage. Whew! The sign saved the day!

Then there was the time when our leading lady came down with a cold just before our single evening performance for the community. Her speaking voice, though nasal, could be heard by the audience with the help of the microphones. Her singing voice was another matter. The viruses had outwitted us, and we had no solution. We just cautioned her to be certain to stand at the mike location for her three solos. The audience knew she was having difficulty, but they understood. Audiences are sympathetic where children's unsolvable problems are concerned.

Once we had a girl who was cast in a secondary lead. Amy had a beautiful voice, yet the script did not call for her to sing at all. We felt that she should have an opportunity to use that fine voice. We went back to the original script, found a song for her that had been omitted in shortening the production and put the song back into the show. It added only about two minutes to the total length of the show, and it was worth it to show off Amy's voice. Another script included a song for a secondary lead. The child who played that part had a beautiful voice, but when she became nervous she lost most of her volume, despite Sandy's exercises. Our solution that time was to make the song into a duet by pairing her with another girl.

If you look hard enough, you can usually find a solution to almost any problem in a show, whether it has to do with music, drama or staging. Children are versatile, and they are usually willing to at least try what you suggest. They know that you will demand of them nothing that will make them look foolish. Always do your best to live up to the trust they have in you.

No Voice Coach

Lest you become discouraged because you have been unable to find a voice coach, be advised that, ten years after Sandy left the show, we are still producing dynamite productions. I have suggested to each of our musical accompanists that they read the "Music" chapter of

This is the way to sell a song.

this book. I cannot force them to use the techniques, however. So, after I make the suggestion, I never mention the book again. Each person must do things the way he or she is most comfortable. You *certainly* don't want to alienate her when she's volunteering her time. Without her, there would be no show.

If we don't have a voice coach, the soloists listen to the tape or compact disc of the show. If we are doing *The Music Man*, for example, the child playing Harold Hill listens to his solos very carefully and practices along with the performers. The group songs are practiced in rehearsals, under my direction. The music teacher may agree to practice with the children in regular music class, also.

In addition to volume and diction in my soloists, I emphasize "Smile!" A happy face will make anyone sound better, or at least the audience will think so. Next time you attend a young people's concert, notice who among the group is smiling and who is not. Your eye is drawn to the smiling faces just like iron shavings to a magnet. You may find yourself smiling right along with the child. I insist that all my soloists and all my actors, both speaking and nonspeaking, smile while on stage except during a serious or a sad scene. Since these are few and far between in a children's show, the "smile" direction prevails.

8

Dance, Finale, and Encore

Dance numbers are another facet of your jewel, the show. Imagine the shining faces of your young performers, the swirling colors of their costumes, the vitality of their feet and arms as they confidently move to the rhythms of the music. At the end of the show, the dancers execute a few of their steps across the stage and are joined by the full cast, dancing and singing. All of the elements of your show build to a visual and musical crescendo, making an unsurpassed finale guaranteed to bring your audience to its feet. The finale is what your audience will remember. Make it smashing and make sure there is a huge smile on each child's face.

If the thought of choreographing a dance gives you a big headache, don't despair. It is not as hard as it seems. The steps must be simple because they will be performed by children, most of whom have no experience in dancing. Planning a dance is well worth the effort because forming a dance group is a great way to amplify the roles of your minor characters. I usually have at least one dance number in every play plus a big finale with dancing and singing. A couple of our shows featured three or four dances in addition to the finale, each performed by a different group of children, and every one was wildly applauded by an enthusiastic audience!

Choreographing the Dance

Reduced to its lowest common denominator, a dance occurs when the dancers enter the stage, move around in an entertaining fashion so that each approaches the front about the same number of times and then exit. At the same time, the dance advances the story a bit and enhances the mood of the show. That statement would put gray hair on the heads of real dancers but the formula works with children.

Perhaps you'll be lucky enough to find a dancer among your parents. For several years I had a set of parents who were quite good at working up simple dance steps in time to the music and teaching them to the children at their home on Saturday mornings and finally on stage at evening rehearsals. Such dedication on the part of these wonderful people is very heartwarming! If you are blessed with such volunteers, take advantage of it.

Usually, however, when you ask for a volunteer to choreograph a dance, most parents head for the nearest exit, frightened of undertaking such a task. You stand a better chance of finding someone willing to *help* you teach the children a dance which is already planned. If that parent has had some previous dance experience, the two of you may be able to work together, revising your routine and perfecting it for the children.

To begin, examine your show to see where a dance might fit as an integral part of your story. Some stories offer obvious opportunities in the form of a ceremony, a wedding or a party with the music built in. We staged one dance to highlight our spectacular Munchkin costumes in *The Wizard of Oz*.

In other shows you may wish to plan the dance around a song. However, singing child-dancers quickly become winded. To avoid the sight of your dancers gasping for air, don't require them to sing as well as dance. They can dance while other children on stage do the singing if lyrics are important to the story. Also, limit the dance to a *maximum* of three minutes. Consider the possibility of highlighting a solo dancer to add a little spice. A solo drummer, if appropriate, is a tremendous help in maintaining rhythm.

Use props in your dance if it seems logical. Just remember to allow plenty of room on stage for dancing with them. In our production of *Annie*, when our nine "orphans" were singing "It's The Hard-Knock Life," each carried a string mop. Sometimes the mops were carried over the shoulder like a rifle; at other times the children industriously mopped the floor. They moved around the floor in a prescribed dance pattern, and wherever they went, their mops went, too. That was one of the most successful dances we ever staged! It even required an encore!

In one production of *Oklahoma!* we had six little girls twirl and

The *Annie* reprise was a smash hit, even without the orphan's mops.

spin umbrellas trimmed in gingham ruffles to match their dresses. In another show six girls executed a maypole dance, twining colorful wide ribbons around the maypole as they maneuvered over and under the arms of their fellow dancers.

Think about the finale, which is different from the dance. Although it may incorporate some of the same style and dance steps, it is shorter, and its purpose is to present the cast to the audience for the bows. It will culminate with the full cast facing the audience and singing the closing song in a final rousing finish.

The greatest limiting factor to the number of dancers in the group may be the size of your stage. It's hard enough to be graceful when you're a fifth grader, but it's even worse when you are bumping into another dancer. Our borrowed stage at the junior high school was 25 × 16 feet and accommodated 24 dancers easily. We used that many dancers on several occasions. A group of any size from three on up may be used.

In *Annie*, Warbucks and Annie danced alone to "I Don't Need Anything But You." The dance ended with Warbucks kneeling on one knee while Annie sat on the other knee. Our Annie was brave enough to put her arm around Warbucks' shoulders. The dance nearly brought down the house!

Consider the style of dance. This is determined by the show, of course. Your dance does not have to be 100 percent authentic in its style. It has only to be sufficiently representative in music, movement and costume to create the proper flavor. That flavor will already be partially established by the story that has gone on before. The audience's imagination will already be on the right track, and what your dance lacks in total authenticity will be filled in by that imagination. For example, in the closing scene of Meredith Willson's *The Music Man*, the town's children must come on stage as a marching band. We didn't happen to have 76 trombones handy or the children to carry them. So we created the impression of a marching band by dressing the children in bright red band uniforms and big smiles and having them march on stage in band formation while belting out "Seventy-six Trombones." No one missed the instruments. The uniforms and singing completely carried the moment and earned the children a standing ovation as the audience clapped in time to the music. It was a moment that gives me goose bumps to this day.

The style of the dance will probably fall into one of the following categories:

➤ Western square, circle or line dance
➤ American Indian dance
➤ Oriental dance
➤ Ballroom dance
➤ Folk dance
➤ Acrobatic, gymnastic, modern style dance

If you are uncertain about precise style, make another trip to the library for books on dances. Check out performances of local dance troupes such as Indian scout groups, Middle Eastern dance groups, etc. Dancers on TV have given me lots of ideas.

Dance Patterns

No matter what style, our dances are built around a few basic patterns used to guide the many pairs of feet through the dance. These include circles, lines, figure eights, crossovers, etc. You, too, can create a dance by combining these basic patterns so that they flow into each other to the tempo of the music. Mix in the flavor and style of your particular dance by altering the way the steps are performed and you have your dance. Presto! Be sure to include a freeze-pause near the end of the dance so that the dancers may accept their well-earned applause before dancing off stage.

Plot your dance on paper. It may resemble the football coach's secret weapon for the all-important Sunday game, with circles and arrows and lots of numbers, but it will help you tremendously to visualize your plan. Time each step or formation to the words of the song you are using so it all comes out even. This is important. Children relate better to words than to rhythm or beat. Give your dance a test run by rounding up a few adults who are good sports and trying it out. A slight adjustment here and there and you will feel you have produced a pretty good dance for your children.

It is best to stay flexible and open-minded at this point. Sometimes what looks good on paper and with adult dancers may fall apart when children try it. Also, what is artistic and appealing from the bird's eye view may be a disaster as seen from the audience's position. This happened to me once. I must have thought my name was Busby Berkeley! Remember the old movies from the 1930s and 1940s? The camera must have been placed on the ceiling to photograph some of those fantastic patterns.

Although you will try to work out as many problems as possible before the dance is presented to the children, there will always be minor changes once you begin to teach the dance. The following pages show some simple, basic patterns you can use to choreograph your dance.

Teaching Children to Dance

There is a simple technique to teaching a dance to children, some of whom haven't a rhythmic cell in their entire bodies. It can be done. The trick is to break the dance down into small parts.

Use no music until the entire dance has been learned. At your first dance rehearsal, line up the children and teach them the basic step of the dance, including both foot and hand movements. In one routine we even had head movements.

Even in a simple march, the idea of starting with the right foot may be hard for some children. There are several ways you can help a child who can't remember. Begin by telling him, "You can do it!"

Dance patterns: entrances

KEY
Stage right dancers X
Stage right line leaders ⊗
Stage left dancers O
Stage left line leaders ◉
Leading characters ⊗
Secondary characters ⊀
Others (nondancers, non-leads) +

Entrances (Reverse for exit)

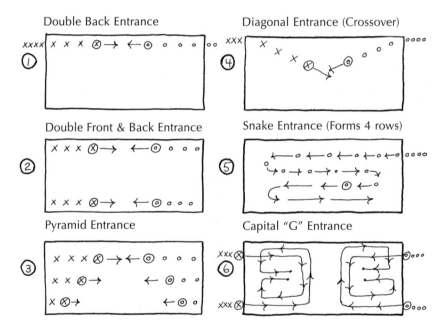

Double Back Entrance

Diagonal Entrance (Crossover)

Double Front & Back Entrance

Snake Entrance (Forms 4 rows)

Pyramid Entrance

Capital "G" Entrance

Give children a challenge and they will rise to it. Then stand next to him and keep trying, or place him in between two confident dancers and ask him to imitate them. The same confusion can occur with hands. I remember a girl who could not instantaneously distinguish between her right and left hand. She was doing a grand-right-and-left routine in a square dance, and she had no time to think. She always stuck out the wrong hand! Solution: I put a bracelet on the hand she was to extend to her partner, and all was well. Practice and practice and practice until it becomes second nature.

Once the feet know exactly what to do, then and only then can

Right-Angle marches

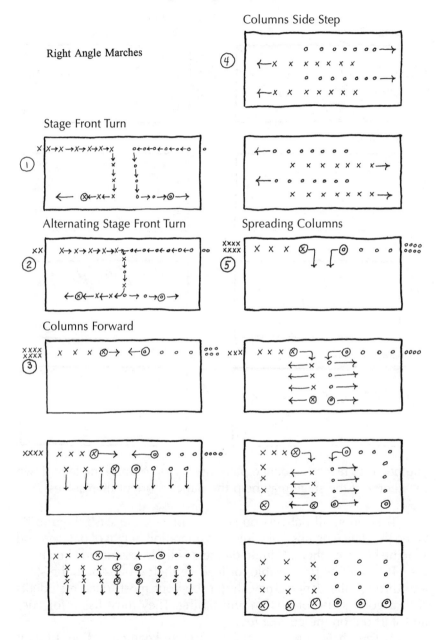

Columns Side Step

Right Angle Marches

Stage Front Turn

Alternating Stage Front Turn

Spreading Columns

Columns Forward

Circle steps

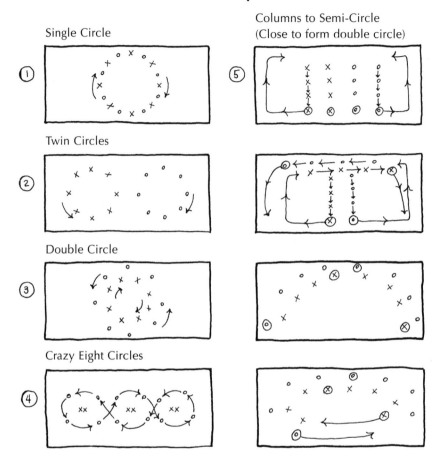

Single Circle

Columns to Semi-Circle
(Close to form double circle)

Twin Circles

Double Circle

Crazy Eight Circles

you begin to teach the dance patterns. A strip of masking tape down the center of the stage may help the dancers orient themselves.

(1) Position all dancers on stage in places you wish them to be when the dance begins. Take into consideration height of dancers and spacing between them. Certain dancers will be designated "line leaders." They will be responsible for leading their groups onto the stage and through the dance. They should be your most reliable students with a good sense of rhythm and timing. They must listen for cues and start out on the correct foot.

(2) Then have the dancers file offstage, keeping in line, to their predance locations in the wings. Have each dancer carefully note his or her lineup position, and make a list for yourself.

Pairs patterns

Pairs Patterns

Box Step
(Step one, feet together)

Virginia Reel Pairs
Boy-girl pairs join hands to form arch. Back-stage pair dance through arch to front and join hands to form arch. Each new backstage couple does the same.

Carousel Step
Boy-girl partners. Boy kneels on one knee, holds girl's hand over his head. She walks around him. Reverse.

Pair Twirl Step
Boy-girl partners hold hands and swing around, facing each other.

(3) Then have the children come back on stage and teach them the first two or three steps of the routine. Repeat the steps several times that day.

(4) At the next rehearsal, review the lineup and the steps learned at the first rehearsal, and then teach the next two or three steps. Practice all of the steps.

Crossover steps

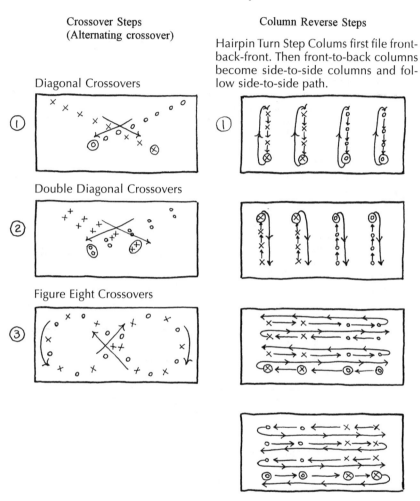

Crossover Steps
(Alternating crossover)

Column Reverse Steps

Hairpin Turn Step Colums first file front-back-front. Then front-to-back columns become side-to-side columns and follow side-to-side path.

Diagonal Crossovers

Double Diagonal Crossovers

Figure Eight Crossovers

(5) The next time, review all the steps, teach the last two or three, and then rehearse the whole dance. Remind the children to SMILE!

If one or two dancers are having difficulty, do not embarrass them by singling them out at rehearsal. Either work with them after rehearsal is over or line up the whole row of dancers and have each one go through the troublesome step.

You may wish for a simple technique that will enable you to see how the groups intertwine and whether they are balanced on stage. For example, if your dancers are divided into four groups and each group is wearing a different color, you will want to be certain that the colors are moving in a balanced fashion across the stage. You can do this easily by having each child hold a large sheet of construction paper matching his group's color. That way, long before costumes are made, you can stand back and note that the reds and greens and yellows and blues are well positioned on stage.

On the day you finally add music to the dance, do not expect things to run smoothly. You will need a patient accompanist, since you may find that your dance does not quite fit the music, despite your best efforts. Work with the dancers and accompanist, adding or subtracting music until it all comes out right.

Once that is done, continue refreshing your dancers' memories by practicing frequently. The first time you add that number to the show rehearsal, around March 1, allow extra time. You will need it.

About two weeks after the children have mastered the dance, they and the rest of the cast should be ready to absorb a new routine, the finale. Teach the finale in the same way as the dance, step by step, but do it during drama rehearsal since it involves the entire cast.

That brings up a major point. When do you hold dance rehearsals? After school you are immersed in drama rehearsals, and you can't be in two places at once. Neither can the children. Usually the dancers have minor, nonspeaking parts or only one or two lines to say. In early February find a location in the school building away from the drama rehearsals. I have used an empty classroom, the school front lobby, even a hallway in which to hold dance rehearsals. You will turn the drama rehearsals over to the assistant director for at least one day a week, so it is important that she have time to watch every section of the play at least once before taking charge.

You are now free to work with the dancers. On previous days they have watched some of their classmates with speaking parts as they practiced their dramatic parts, and they are most anxious to have their turn. I usually have several parents who have volunteered to be "dance teachers" and have taught them the dance at a prearranged time. So, after several days of dance rehearsals, I turn that operation over to my wonderful parent volunteers, and I return to drama rehearsals. I remember a time when I had three rehearsals going at once: drama, dance 1, and dance 2. I have even held dance rehearsals at 8:00 A.M.—*if* I had a reliable group who wouldn't forget to come to school early. When the dancers join drama rehearsals around March 1, I am able to smooth out any rough spots and work on entrances and exits.

One of the dance routines that was most popular with our audience was a segment we picked up when we attended a high school production of an entirely different play than the one we were doing. When we saw how the audience loved it, we simply had to incorporate it into our show. This is how it went. In the middle of the dance, four boys lay down on their backs, feet toward the audience, evenly spaced across the stage. Their feet were on the floor and their knees were bent. Four other dancers knelt across these boys' hips, with one knee on each side of the prone child. The prone child kicked first one foot up high, and then the other, as the upright child lifted both arms, first to one side of his body, then to the other. It appeared to the audience that the upright dancer was performing amazing gymnastic feats. The audience loved it!

I have been asked if we ever audition dancers. We did this once. For *Annie* we decided that our dance number would be based on the Charleston and performed by the people living in "Hooverville." For children with no dance experience, the Charleston is quite a challenge! The children interested in being dancers were taught some Charleston steps about two weeks before regular auditions were scheduled. We

A spectacular finale for *Annie Get Your Gun.*

intended to have them perform the steps during their audition. About three days later I noticed that our "dancers" were teaching the steps to our "nondancers." Before Audition Day arrived every fifth-grade child knew how to do the Charleston. Some were better than others, but all of them knew the steps! At recess I would see little groups of children on the playground, all doing the Charleston. I looked up one day and found three boys working on the steps in a back corner of the classroom instead of doing their math assignment! As it turned out, our audience loved the dance as much as the children did.

Sample Dance

To demonstrate how the patterns, style and diagrams can be blended for a specific show, let's consider a dance for Rodgers and Hammerstein's *Oklahoma!* (See page 102.) Naturally, the cast will be belting out a rousing rendition of the title song. The perfect choice for a dance style is square dancing, as popular in the early part of this century as it is now. Even simpler for children to perform is a round dance formation using some square dancing steps.

(1) At the sound of the first notes, two lines of children enter from the back corners of the stage, one from the right and one from the left.

(2) They move toward the center back of the stage, then forward and around until they have formed two circles. They are holding hands in a chain fashion as they enter. When the circles are formed, each will circle left for several measures of music, then circle right for several measures.

(3) Children then stop and face each other in partners around each circle.

(4) Each child in partnership extends his right hand, taking his partner's right hand, and proceeds to "Grand Right and Left" around the circle, using right hand, left hand, right hand, etc. The line leader's path is indicated on page 96, under "Circle steps."

(5) When the child is back to his original partner, partners join hands and skip around the circle.

(6) When all partners reach their original places, all children join hands and move to the center of the circle, hands up.

(7) Then they move back to their original places, lowering hands.

(8) Next the child who led the right line on stage originally now leads the circle across the back of the stage and around until a line is formed across the front of the stage.

Oklahoma! dance patterns

Oklahoma!

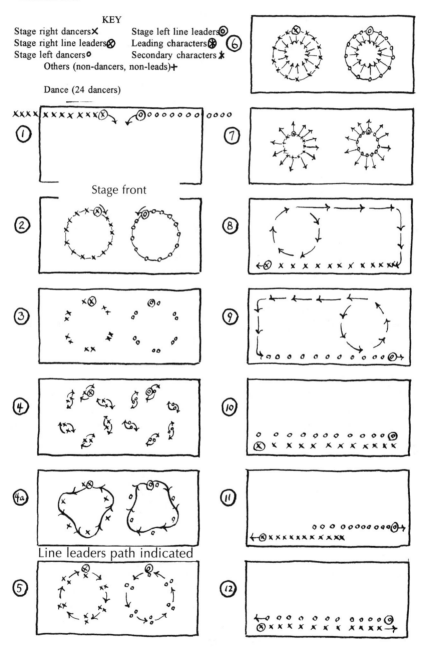

KEY

Stage right dancers ✗
Stage right line leaders ⊗
Stage left dancers ○
Stage left line leaders ◎
Leading characters ✪
Secondary characters ✶
Others (non-dancers, non-leads) ✚

Dance (24 dancers)

Stage front

Line leaders path indicated

(9) The other circle on stage does the same routine, but its line goes in the reverse direction, ending up in the back of the first line.

(10) Now you have two lines across the stage, one in front of the other.

(11) Have each line move, sidestepping, in one direction. The front line moves right, and the back line moves left, for four steps.

(12) Then the lines reverse direction for four steps until both are back in their original position.

Finale and Encore

At this point the dance could easily become the finale number in one of two ways. First, see illustration titled "Finale A:"

(1) The children with lead parts who are not dancers have been standing to the side fronts of the stage, singing and clapping in time to the music.

(2) They now move into place, in a line in front of the two dancing lines.

(3) They should stand with the leading lady and the leading man in the center of the stage, the secondary leads on either side of them, and so on in descending order of importance of parts. They finish singing the song with the entire cast on stage.

(4) Nondancers and nonleads will form a line behind the dancers. At the last note and shout of "Oklahoma! Okay!" the entire cast raises its right arm.

Now see "Finale B":

(1) The two rows of dancers split in the center by taking two side steps toward their respective sides of the stage, forming a center aisle.

(2) The leads enter the stage from the back and walk up the aisle toward the audience in ascending order of importance.

(3) They will alternately turn right or left at stage front, forming a line in front of the dancers, with the leading lady and leading man in the center.

(4) Nondancers and nonleads will line up behind the dancers. The final note is sung and right arms shoot up in unison. Applause!

After the thunderous applause dies down, you must be prepared to go into an encore. Encores don't just happen; actors are prepared

Oklahoma! finale patterns

KEY
Stage right dancers **X**
Stage right line leaders ⊗
Stage left dancers **O**
Stage left line leaders ⊙
Leading characters ⊗
Secondary characters ✶
Others (nondancers, non-leads) +

Finale A

Finale B

for them, so you must teach the children what to do. Here's how (see page 105):

(1) As the first musical notes are heard, the leading actors and actresses in the front row and other nondancers in the back row will quickly move to their respective sides of the stage.

(2) As the singing begins again, the front row of dancers turns and goes to the right of the stage while the second row goes left.

(3) Both rows turn at the side curtain and proceed to the back of

Oklahoma! encore patterns

Encore

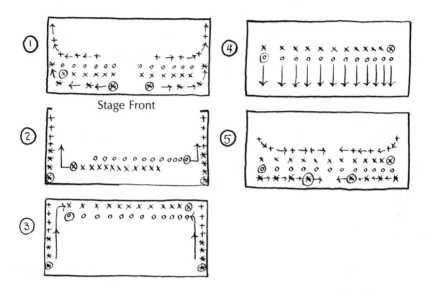

Stage Front

the stage. They turn again toward the center and once again form two lines, but this time the second row will be in front and the first row in the back. This will make the parents of row two dancers very happy.

(4) Both rows move toward the front of the stage.

(5) The leading characters move back to their positions for bows as the song ends again. Now bask in the warmth of the applause and get ready for your well-earned bows.

For our shows we try to have a rousing opening scene, usually with a song. We like to end the same way—with a smashing, ear-jingling song, accompanied by some type of colorful dance or marching routine. Your audience is always left with a particular impression of the show, and all other feelings seem to pale beside the one they experience at the finale. Capitalize on that fact, and do your best to involve the entire cast in an outstanding closing number. It's good theater, and you above all are striving for a smash hit!

9

Costumes and Makeup

Costumes help to transform the children into the characters they portray and are a great source of excitement. Begin work on your costumes *early*, as soon as the winter holidays are over. That allows three months to prepare for an early April performance. Our children are responsible for supplying and paying for their own costumes. The parents are quite willing to assume these costs, and this arrangement enables the children to keep the costumes as souvenirs after the show is over.

If a child's costume is unique to the character she is playing, then it is created entirely by the child and her family. We do not become involved other than to suggest the costume's basic design based on our knowledge of the show and its time period. For example, if a child is to be a cowboy in *Oklahoma!*, he will probably wear jeans, a plaid shirt with collar and a cowboy hat. The child and his parent are responsible for choosing the shirt and cowboy hat without any guidance from us. Usually, though, we are able to order inexpensive cowboy hats in bulk, and the child has the option of placing an order with us. Some of our parents in the past have chosen to purchase cowboy boots for their sons, but this is an expensive choice and is not required.

A general description of costumes is an important part of the audition announcement sent home in the fall. If the costume must exactly match others in fabric and pattern, then the fabric is purchased in bulk and the costumes are cut from master patterns. Parents pay for the fabric and sew their child's costume themselves. Occasionally after the show families will generously choose to donate the outfit to the Costume Closet for the benefit of future casts. For most, however, the souvenir value far outweighs anything else.

Costume Coordinator

JoAnn, our costume coordinator, begins planning for costumes during September and October, approximately six months before the performance. She checks pattern catalogs at fabric stores, particularly the costume section at the back of the book, to locate patterns that can be adapted for our use. She notes pattern numbers so that she can pass this information on to parents. When identical outfits must be made for a group of children, she purchases the pattern in perhaps two sizes most common to our children, from which master patterns can be drawn. JoAnn chairs the Costume Committee, pairing sewing volunteers with nonsewing parents so that each child is handsomely decked out in time for the show. She works closely with the director on the many details.

It is not necessary for your costume coordinator to be a seamstress. JoAnn doesn't even own a sewing machine. The few times she has wanted a basic garment for the children to try on for size, she has done all the sewing by hand. Her creativity, however, *far* outweighs any advantage sewing ability might have given her. She has tacked gold foil fringe to the bottoms of the green Emerald City residents' costumes in *The Wizard of Oz*. She has designed dancers' costumes that are suggestive of can-can girls but are entirely appropriate for ten-year-old girls.

One practical reason to begin work on costumes early is to avoid the pitfalls of seasonal fabric. The perfect fabric you found in October may no longer be available when you get around to purchasing it in late February. If it has to be ordered, it could take many weeks if it is available at all. In our production of *Annie Get Your Gun*, our 19 Indian dancers wore outfits made of a rust-colored velour that looked to the audience like buckskin but was much less expensive than the real thing. According to our plan, each child would pay for his own costume, but in order for the fabric of each to match, we decided to purchase it all at one time on the bolt. I computed the cost and notified the parents, who then sent in the money. When we went to the store in mid–February to purchase the fabric, we found that we had waited too long. Velour is a winter fabric. Stores were selling out and not ordering more. Although they still had short pieces of velour, none seemed to have 56 yards in the color we needed. The large *amount* we needed caused the problem. Eventually we were able to purchase the fabric, but we could have saved ourselves much worry if we had attended to it earlier. You have now learned an important lesson from our mistake.

Keeping Costs Down

Cost is as important a consideration as design in costuming your young cast. Remember that these are children, not professional actors. Their parents are willing to spend reasonable amounts of money on costumes and fabric, but an excess amount is understandably frowned upon. Also, be conscious of the number of costume changes, each of which will add to the total cost. Parents are happiest when stage clothing can be put to a practical use after the show. Minor characters in our play usually wear the same basic outfits for the entire play. The exception is specialty numbers like the Indian dance in *Annie Get Your Gun*, when our cowboys and ladies doubled as Indian dancers. In that show our girls with minor parts were dressed in long skirts and high-necked blouses for most of the play. The skirts could be cut off later and combined with the blouses to make pretty school ensembles. The boys with minor parts wore regular pants and either cowboy shirts or dress shirts with collars instead of crew or turtle necks. We added string ties and straw hats or cowboy hats to a few boys for stage interest. All of the outfits were practical, everyday clothing that could be used later, so the parents did not object to purchasing fabric for the Indian dance costumes, even though their future use was probably limited to pajamas or Halloween costumes.

The term "low cost" means different things to different people. All of our royal children in *The King and I* used the same pattern for their costumes, a floor-length A-line tunic with long sleeves. The fabric varied, though, according to the choice of the parents. Some used silky fabric usually used for linings of garments. Others used brightly colored satins. Still others used very ornate brocades. All were trimmed with the same gold braid down the center front. Their hats will be discussed later.

In *The Wizard of Oz*, Glenda's costume had to communicate the idea that she was good yet still a witch. Our little actress's mother made a costume out of white fabric and added a sequined cape to go with it. JoAnn, our costume coordinator, purchased a witch's hat for Glenda and then covered the entire hat with white fabric. Glenda was dressed exactly right, and no one could miss her character representation. (See page 110.)

Costumes for the main characters always seem to be an entirely different matter from those for the rest of the cast. Our lead characters usually need two or three apparel changes. Parents of lead and secondary lead characters are willing to spend more money on costumes than those whose children have minor parts. No matter how I consider cost, these parents are always willing to go beyond the call of duty in providing their children with wonderfully lavish regalia. Of course, those extravagant duds emphasize the importance of the main characters and add immeasurably to the success of the show. The mother of our leading man in one production of *Annie Get Your Gun* made him a white satin cowboy shirt with six-inch silk fringe attached to the front and back yokes. She then made a reversible vest, black velvet on one side and red satin on the other. By adding his vest and then turning it inside out between scenes, he could totally change the look of his costume. She purchased a pair of black pants and black cowboy boots to complete his outfit. She topped the whole thing off with a black cowboy hat bedecked with a white jeweled band. Our Frank Butler was magnificent thanks to the generosity of his mom.

No costumes can surpass those of our "Mrs. Anna" in *The King and I*. She had two costumes, both worn over a hoop skirt. The child's mother couldn't buy a hoop skirt for a small child, so she borrowed an adult one, took it entirely apart, and made it over to fit her daughter. (Of course, she re-made it for the adult before she returned it to its owner when the show was over.) The girl's first costume was a light blue dress with white collar, cuffs, and belt and a very full skirt. A short blue cape was worn over her shoulders, and she had a matching blue hat. The cape and hat were worn in the first scene, when she was arriving in Siam. The dress alone was perfect for the classroom as she taught the royal children. The showstopper, though, was her party dress! The child's mother designed it to look similar to the one worn by Mrs. Anna on the cover of the record album. It was exquisite! See the picture of the costume on the front cover of this book, as words will not do it justice.

The king's costumes were just as elaborate. In one outfit his pants were black satin, and his top was green and gold with one-inch gold trim down both sides of the center front, open to show his chest. His party costume was red satin pants paired with a red and gold brocade tunic. The top was trimmed with heavily beaded 1 1/2-inch wide trim down the center front. Here was certainly an example of a parent sparing no expense to costume her son as the king!

Mix a little imagination with some good old-fashioned borrow-

Glenda, the Good Witch, in *The Wizard of Oz*.

ing and you will be able to create many costumes at absolutely no cost. Millions of outfits lie in dusty attics of this fair land. Others languish in thrift shops. Spread the word about what you need. For a particularly hard-to-find item, run an ad in your PTA newsletter.

Long skirts always seem to be plentiful. We have been able to borrow a sport coat for a boy who does not own one. Even if the loaned items are not perfect sizes for your children, often they can be tucked in here and there to make them fit. If the item is donated outright, take it apart and remake it for the child if necessary. In one of our shows, we had a pixie of a girl playing the part of a little boy. We borrowed a shirt for her from one of the boys in the cast. Someone donated a pair of outgrown pants, so we cut them off below the knee, gathered in the leg at the cut-off point with elastic and made a perfect pair of knickers.

The one area where your imagination may fail you is shoes, the

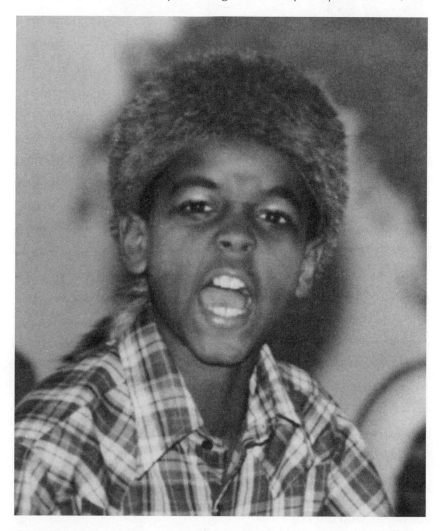

Hats like these could be gathering dust in an attic. Ask around! You never know what you'll find.

Elegantly dressed for a party, Mrs. Anna and the King waltz to "Shall we Dance?" Self-confidence wears its own magic.

hardest item to find. Children these days live in sneakers, and many do not own dress shoes. Sneakers simply do not look appropriate for the time periods in many plays. Of course, Indians and urchins can always go barefooted unless your stage is splintery. Sometimes in desperation we have borrowed dress shoes from children who had them for others who did not.

Ballet slippers can be used, and they are a handy addition to your costume closet. Ask parents to think of you when it is time to discard old ballet slippers. Contact the local ballet school and ask for donations. Put an ad in that PTA newsletter. Check thrift shops. I have worked hard to build up the supply of ballet slippers in our costume closet. Some of them are used in every single show.

Advertise within your school community for needed items. If your parents are aware of the types of outfits you are collecting, gradually your costume closet will grow into a gold mine of classic garments. Certain items, such as petticoats, long skirts and high-necked blouses will be used again and again. We have an admirable assortment of hats for both sexes. We also collect old jewelry, especially brooches, which lend authenticity to period costumes when pinned to the high neck of a blouse. A large necklace that can be looped around the top of a coat hanger with the costume backstage and then popped over the head of the actress is satisfactory. Otherwise, use jewelry that can be permanently pinned to the costume. Avoid that which must be removed or added during the course of the play, particularly small pieces and earrings that are easily lost backstage.

Hats

What a magical accessory is the lowly hat! It can convey the idea of a particularly hard-to-find costume with ease. JoAnn, our costume coordinator, is a master with hats!

One of the loveliest and most inventive hats ever made was also the most hilarious. In *Annie Get Your Gun* Annie Oakley shoots a stuffed bird decoration off the hat of Dolly Tate. We decided the most sensible way to handle this trick was to allow Dolly to appear on stage wearing the hat with the bird perched on top. Then she would exit stage left, a shot would be heard, and Annie would enter stage right, looking around for the bird she had just shot. Dolly, outraged, marches on from the opposite side of the stage, still wearing the hat, but carrying the bird in her hand. There is no pause in the action. One thing happens right after the other. That bird had to be instantly removable when Dolly came off stage so that she could come back on immediately with the bird in her hand.

JoAnn, costume designer extraordinaire, applied her genius to the challenge and came up with the perfect solution. She found a black straw hat with medium brim. She purchased a large white dove at Christmas time, when such items were available. She sewed a circle of half-inch wide elastic to the crown of the hat and slipped the dove

Annie Oakley (left) and Dolly Tate, from *Annie Get Your Gun*. (Photo: Jim Tingstrum, *Journal Newspapers*.)

into it. To hide the elastic, decorate the hat and also keep the hat on the child's head, she used white nylon netting. It made a pretty "nest" for the bird, hiding the elastic at the crown, and was pulled over the brim and tied under Dolly's chin in a big bow. Dolly wore the hat in the first part of the scene, bird in elastic. When she exited and the shot was heard, the bird was quickly slipped out of the elastic and Dolly rushed back on stage carrying it. The audience loved it!

The royal children in *The King and I* presented another problem. All 25 of them needed "crowns" of some sort, including Chulalongkorn, the crown prince. JoAnn cut out 25 strips of tagboard measuring about 4 × 12 inches, and stapled each into a cylinder. She purchased gold lame fabric by the yard and cut and sewed 25 pieces to cover the tagboard cylinders, gathering the edges at center top and center bottom. A piece of elastic thread was attached to each so the child could put it under his chin, thus keeping the hat in place. (See page 116.)

Parents are creative, too. The nuns in *The Sound of Music* needed authentic-looking head coverings, and one kind volunteer made them all. In *The Wizard of Oz*, the audience *loved* the hat of the Mayor of Munchkinville, fashioned by the child's mother. Chief Sitting Bull's headdress in *Annie Get Your Gun* was purchased unassembled, and it took two parents about three hours to put it together! (See page 116.)

For *Annie*, JoAnn constructed hats for our Hooverville Charleston dancers. Each was a circle of tagboard or poster board about 18 inches in diameter. She cut a hole in each to fit the crown of the child's head, and then covered the entire "hat" with newspaper. (Hooverville folks were very poor and used newspaper inside their clothes for insulation on cold nights.) Next she made large newspaper flowers and glued them around the hat. Each hat was held on a child's head by an elastic thread under the chin. Those hats bounced and gyrated as our Charleston dancers displayed their fancy footwork. The entire effect was smashing!

Then there was the nonhat. The girl who played the part of a backwoods maiden had long dark hair. She wore her hair in braids that stood out from either side of her head. To make the braids, I straightened out a coat hanger, bent the center to fit the shape across the top of her head to the ears, and then bent each end up and out. The part of the hanger that sat on her head didn't show from the stage. For the other parts of the hanger, I used each side as a base, and braided her hair to cover the hanger. I did this on each side of her head. The effect was her pigtails standing straight up and out. It was hilarious!

In *Annie*, the girl who played the title role had brown hair instead of the traditional red hair associated with this character. So she curled her hair. Each night her mother put it up in rags, so it would form long finger curls when it was taken down. Annie's hair was very distinctive and was a nice substitute for the red color.

Specialty Accessories

Some plays require specialty costume items for which a pattern will not be available. Such an item were the spats we wanted for the boys in *The Music Man*. A brave parent volunteered to make a pattern for us. Using scraps of fabric and the trial-and-error method, she finally succeeded. She sent the pattern to me, and I duplicated it and sent it home to the parents. They made spats and matching bow ties, and our boys looked great!

Sometimes, though, you simply can't make what you need. The only solution is to purchase, but at as cheap a price as possible. I located two companies that carried many of the specialty items we needed. Remember those cowboy hats we purchased in bulk at a very inexpensive price? We ordered them through a catalog. Another time we

Examples of creative headwear. *Top left:* Crown Prince Chulalongkorn in *The King and I; top right:* Tin Woodman in *The Wizard of Oz; bottom left:* Mayor of Munchkinville in *The Wizard of Oz; bottom right:* Chief Sitting Bull in *Annie Get Your Gun.*

needed a tiara. We ordered it through a catalog. We usually dealt with one of two companies. I'm sure they would send you their catalogs if you request them.

1) U.S. Toy Co., Inc., 2008 West 103rd Terrace, Leawood, KS 66206.
2) Oriental Trading Company, P.O. Box 3407, Omaha, NE 68103-0407, phone 1-800-228-2269.

For *Annie Get Your Gun*, we found a spectacular Indian head-dress and also a bear claw necklace in the Boy Scout catalog.

Hoop Skirts and Petticoats

The King and I was set in the hoop-skirt era. Our ladies needed them. The hoop-skirts rage of the fifties had come and gone, and we could not locate a single hoop. Fortunately, the physical education teacher in our school had among her athletic equipment a number of large plastic "Hula Hoops." She was not using them in her classes at the time, so she loaned them to us for two months. A very creative gal on our Costume Committee turned them into hoop skirts. She cut long strips of fabric from old bed sheets and attached six strips evenly around an elastic waistband. The other end of the strips was looped around the hoop and sewn in place at ankle length. Presto! Hoop skirts! A word of caution, though. If you choose to use this idea, be sure to tell your girls to stand well away from anyone or anything else. If the child backs into something, that hoop, being so rigid, will flip right up in front, showing whatever the young lady is wearing underneath! Of course, if she is wearing pantalets, no harm will be done, and it will surely earn a laugh from the audience.

One valuable addition to our costume closet was petticoats made from nylon netting. They are used year after year. Using funds donated by the PTA, we purchased 24 yards of white nylon netting, 36 inches wide. Ten-year-old girls are not very tall, and because we used a dropped-hip style, each petticoat required a small amount of netting. The netting was cut in half lengthwise. One-inch elastic served as the waistband to which was attached a 12-inch band of old bedsheet muslin. The netting was gathered and stitched to the bottom of the sheeting. Had the netting been attached directly to the elastic waistband, not only would we have been limited to fewer petticoats, but they would have felt extremely scratchy to the girls as well. There have been occasions when I have wished that there was twice as much netting in each petticoat, making it stand out better, but that's a matter for your budget.

Color Can Do Wonders

When planning costumes, think of color and how it interacts with the backdrop and other actors' clothing. Remember that costumes

Hoop skirts and petticoats made from one-inch elastic, old bedsheets, hoops and netting

are blocks of color as seen by the audience, so let them do the work of creating the illusion you desire. Children who play parts of older characters should be dressed in darker colors, whereas those who play young people are dressed in bright colors.

Your male and female leads should be dressed in vivid colors so that they stand out from the other characters. Take care during the early planning stages that the colors chosen for your leads do not clash. The sight of the leading lady dressed in hot pink gazing into the eyes of the leading man dressed in burnt orange could be somewhat jarring. How much better it would be for her to be dressed in blue or pale green. Once we almost had two male secondary leads dressed in identical light blue. One parent thought of this in the nick of time and bought electric blue fabric instead, so we avoided the Blue Twins.

We reserve the color red for our leading lady or leading man. No other child may have a costume this color. For the final scene, we don't want *both* of them to appear in red. To avoid any costume "glitches" between these two characters, their parents should discuss and plan colors in advance.

During one dress rehearsal when we saw the finished costumes all together for the first time, we found that most of the minor characters were dressed in white tops, girls in white blouses and boys in white shirts. They did not fade into the backdrop, but they did look like they all shopped at the same dull clothing store. White can be drab when used on stage in quantity. At that late date, we hurriedly rounded up some bright scarfs and sashes for the girls. We added colorful ties to the boys' costumes. That was the best we could do on short notice to remedy a problem we did not realize we had until it was almost too late. From then on we encouraged our casts to choose colored blouses and shirts, and now there is always a pleasing color mix.

A single hue worn by many dancers on stage makes a big impact so we try to choose a main color for the backdrop that will be harmonious with the dancers' costumes. In addition to the backdrop, be conscious of the shade of the curtains on your stage. One year the junior high school, whose stage we were using, threw away their old neutral beige stage curtains and installed new ones that were a deep midnight blue, a big change! If our children had worn very dark costumes on that stage, they would have been invisible to the audience when viewed against those curtains. Luckily, we knew about this new addition long before the costumes were made, and we were able to advise parents to avoid dark colors.

In the movie version of *The Wizard of Oz* the Munchkins are very short people, to distinguish them from Dorothy, the witch, the Cowardly Lion, Tinman and Scarecrow. When one produces that play using all ten-year-olds, most of whom are the same height, how does one make the Munchkins look different? Again, our extraordinary costume coordinator came up with the solution: multicolored wigs! To go along with the wigs, the costumes were also outlandishly colorful. We used the neon colors of green, yellow, pink and orange. Each costume used all four colors, but in different combinations. The collar was one color, the bodice another color, a wide strip of a third color was sewn along the bottom of the bodice, and the short skirt (girls) or shorts (boys) were of a fourth color. This may sound like all costumes were made alike. Wrong. One child wore a green collar, yellow bodice with pink band around the bottom, and orange skirt. Another child had a pink collar, green bodice with orange band, and yellow shorts. In other words, the colors were all sewn in different places. With the multicolored (blue, yellow and red) wigs, our Munchkins surely stood out from the others! You should have heard the audience when these characters came on stage for the first time!

Our orphans in *Annie* are another story. The first time we did the show, they were allowed to wear any old, scroungy clothes they had. Ten years later, when we performed that show again, the orphans were dressed in uniforms—drab maroon A-line dresses with colorful patches sewn on, and at least ten inches of white bloomers showing below the dress. Believe me, the uniforms were *much* more effective!

In *The Music Man* we were looking for some way to make our

barbershop quartet stand out. Our costume coordinator clothed each of them in white pants and a gingham vest with a "skimmer" hat sporting a matching gingham hat band. Each member of the quartet wore a different color of gingham. The effect was just what we had been looking for.

While we are on the subject of *The Music Man,* our 24 River City Band members wore black pants and red taffeta tunics with a mandarin collar and gold braid down the center. Completing the outfit were matching spats and a tall red cylinder hat trimmed in the same gold braid and with black bill. When those children, decked out in those red tunics, marched around the stage and did their intricate dance patterns while belting out "Seventy-six Trombones," they received a standing ovation from their audience! Talk about a spectacular finale! It *still* brings tears to my eyes!

The Quick Change

The last consideration in costume design is the ease and speed with which the attire can be changed. The tempo of your play must never be slowed by a long pause for costume changes. Consider, too, that backstage is often a dark, cramped space with little room for mass costume changing, let alone modesty. For characters who wear the same basic outfit throughout the play, this is not a problem. However, for the leading lady who must be transformed from a dirty little waif into a high-fashion society lady in under one minute, it becomes very important indeed.

Use every device you can think of to simplify the change and meet this challenge. Accessories can be a clever answer. The look of a simple costume can be totally changed by using many different accessories such as shawls, capes, vests, hats, sashes, ties, purses, scarves, aprons, collars, etc. Remember the reversible vest worn by our Frank Butler in *Annie Get Your Gun.* Such items are a boon to harried backstage help.

The heroine Maria in Rodgers and Hammerstein's *The Sound of Music* began the show at the abbey wearing her novice's uniform, consisting of a simple gray dress with a white apron and black veil. For the next scene, when she appears at the Von Trapp's front door, we would remove the apron and veil and add an old jacket to create her drab little outfit.

Eventually Maria had to change out of that gray dress. If it had

had 50 tiny buttons down the back we would have been in trouble! Even if your backstage crew has the dexterity of an octopus, buttons can be a nightmare. Ties are all right; zippers are even better. Velcro is also a blessing to costume changing. If you *must* use buttons, make sure they are big.

Take a tip from mountain climbers and use the layering technique. That way one outfit can be quickly removed to reveal another. It is much easier to snatch off costume no. 1 over the leading lady's head at the end of scene one and immediately send her out for scene two wearing costume no. 2 than to strip her down to her underwear between scenes. This works well as long as the first costume is looser, bulkier and slightly longer than the second. Our leading lady in *Annie Get Your Gun* started the show wearing a burlap gathered skirt and tan peasant blouse. Hidden under that was her next outfit, a white blouse and red velour skirt and matching vest, both trimmed with six-inch white silk fringe. When the time came to change, she had only to pull off the burlap skirt and peasant blouse, put on her cowboy boots and pop the red cowboy hat trimmed with white feathers on her head. Think how much longer it would have taken her to put on the whole red outfit, too.

In a later scene, our Annie Oakley had to wear a fancy party dress. She ducked behind a three-cornered screen that we kept backstage for her costume changes and shed her red skirt, vest, hat and boots. To her white blouse she added a long white skirt, shoes and a scoop-necked sleeveless top covered with pearl sequins. The top was one of those treasures we uncovered in someone's attic and had trimmed to fit our Annie. A red taffeta sash loaded with her medals draped from one shoulder to the opposite hip. This elegance was topped off by a rhinestone tiara loaned by another parent. Our Annie's costume glittered as much as her performance!

In the same show, our cowboys and ladies were able to transform themselves into Indian dancers while confined to a small coed territory backstage and maintain modesty at the same time. The Indian costumes consisted of loosely fitting long-sleeved tops and full-length pants. The boys simply slipped the suits over their cowboy outfits. The girls, who were all dressed in blouses and long skirts, first put the Indian tops on over their blouses. Then they pulled the pants on under their skirts and removed the skirts. An Indian headband for each dancer was packed with the costume. Changing was a fast operation, and the system worked well except for the first dress rehearsal. On that day the scene began too soon and the lead dancer appeared on stage with his Indian pants in his hand to a chorus of giggles from onlookers. After that the backstage crew always made sure everyone was completely in costume before the scene was allowed to begin.

Picture this: a dark backstage area. Nineteen Indian costumes hanging on hangers, waiting to be donned when the time came. Whose costume was whose? They were all alike! I cut tagboard nametags (2 × 5 inches), printed each child's name on one in thick black marker, and attached it to the hook of the hanger on which his costume hung. I felt so smart! As dress rehearsals and performances progressed, however, name tags became lost. Finally there were fewer than ten tags left on hangers. Yet the children magically appeared on stage, each in his or her own costume! I'll never know how they managed that!

Costume Committee

Although the mechanics of costuming a play are not difficult, a Costume Committee is essential. The reason is that some parents do not sew, and they will need help making costumes for their children. These parents are generally hesitant even to purchase fabric for fear of choosing the wrong thing. The happy solution to this situation is that a seamstress on the committee agrees to "adopt" a child whose parent does not sew. This adoption entails the purchasing, making and fitting of a costume for the child. The child's parent pays the seamstress directly for fabric and supplies. No charge is made for the loving labor involved in sewing, although one grateful father presented his child's seamstress with a bottle of fine wine.

The second important function of the Costume Committee is cutting fabric from master patterns when many identical costumes are needed, as for a dance group. If your show requires such outfits, the saga of our Indian dance may help you organize the project. For *Annie Get Your Gun* we planned to feature 17 minor characters plus one solo dancer and a drummer in an Indian dance number. We wanted them all dressed in identical costumes. As dancers they needed suits that would allow them free movement and withstand the stresses dancing would place on the seams. They had to be loose enough to fit over and hide their other costumes, which would be worn during the rest of the show. JoAnn, our costume coordinator, found a pattern that seemed to fill the bill. It had a loosely fitting top with long, raglan sleeves and a drawstring neck. The pants were a loose pajama style with an elastic waistband. Both top and pants were trimmed with two-inch self-fringe. We would buy 19 Indian headbands with single feathers. After checking with the scenery chairman about colors to be used in the backdrop, we chose a rust-colored velour fabric that could pass for buckskin.

The first step was to determine how many yards of the velour we would need. In measuring all the children we found that most were fairly close to two standard sizes. A few would need slightly longer sleeves or pant legs. We were careful to measure the sleeve length from shoulder to wrist on the outside, with the arm bent, so that the sleeve would not be too short. JoAnn purchased the Indian patterns and traced them onto brown wrapping paper in two sizes using the originals as a guide. Then on a gridded cutting board, marking off the expected fabric width, she experimented with placement of the two patterns. She found the arrangement that allowed the pieces to fit as closely together as possible and resulted in the least fabric waste. She then measured the length of the section of the cutting board covered by a pattern. She multiplied by the number of costumes needed, and added two extra yards to allow a margin for error. Her calculations came to 56 yards and proved to be quite accurate.

We then entered into the period of fabric search mentioned earlier in this chapter when we discovered what a headache seasonal fabric can be. By the time the Costume Committee gathered for the "cutting bee" at the home of the costume coordinator, we were all acutely aware of what a precious commodity our velour was, and we dared not waste a single scrap. Within two hours, ten mothers wielding shears had cut out 19 costumes and miles of fringe. Each set of costume pieces was packed with a copy of sewing instructions in a plastic bag and labeled with the dancer's name. Thread was not included. The next day those children whose parents could sew were given their costume bags. Those bags intended for children of non-sewing parents were held by the Costume Committee to be made by them. An extra bonus was the fun everyone had. During the course of that delightful evening, several parents who had arrived as strangers had the chance to become acquainted with the parents of their children's friends. The play thus paid another dividend to the community.

Non–English-Speaking Parents

As the years passed, more and more of our student body was foreign born. The children learned English quickly, but their parents often did not. When it came to making costumes for their children, we found that many of these parents could not read the sewing directions, which were written in English. The parents were very hesitant to call on the Costume Committee for help because they could sew. The parents devised several solutions. Some had their children read the sewing instructions to them, one step at a time. Others asked a friend to sew the costume for them. In some cases we were able to embellish our sewing instructions with many more pictures and diagrams than would have ordinarily been used. Once, when the predominance of our non–English parents were Korean, we asked a bilingual parent to write translated instructions for us. We had no idea what we were asking of this kind soul! That job took her hours upon hours and page after page after page of paper! Many parents were very grateful to her, as I was, but I was also embarrassed that I had asked for so much of her time!

Makeup

Stage makeup is a must. Even the newscasters on television must wear it for without it, under the bright lights, they would appear washed out. Children also look pale on stage, so plan to use makeup. During the early months of planning for the show, I always notify my boys that they must wear it, just as the girls do. It takes them some time to get used to the idea. Eventually, they decide that if it's good enough for their heroes on television, it's good enough for them. I really think that more than a few of them are secretly thrilled with the idea. They can pretend masculine disgust and at the same time satisfy a secret yearning to find out what it's like, what women find so appealing about it. Some of them are amazed, when they look in the mirror, by the difference it makes in their looks.

Even though our makeup is kept fairly simple, the children are too young to apply it to themselves. At the parents' meeting recruit volunteers for the Makeup Committee who will apply the cosmetics in assembly-line fashion before the dress rehearsals and before all performances. One parent should head the committee and handle scheduling. You will probably need six to eight parents to handle the job for 35 to 45 children at each performance. Older teenage sisters love to help out for the evening performances.

Cosmetics are expensive. If yours is a no-budget production, send the parents a list of your specific makeup needs and ask them to send in makeup they have but do not want. You'll be pleasantly surprised at the number of donations you'll receive. When you graduate to a small budget, you can purchase whatever you need. Watch newspaper ads for cosmetic sales. Take advantage of less expensive brands carried by most drug stores.

The makeup we usually use is (1) face powder, (2) blush or rouge, (3) lipstick, (4) eye shadow and (5) eyeliner.

Two or three compacts of pressed powder in a rosy tint will be adequate for a half dozen performances. If the powder is donated, buy new inexpensive powder puffs. Put no powder on African American and other dark-skinned children unless you have appropriate shades. The powder you use for white-skinned children looks chalky and unattractive on those with darker skin.

Use the powder type of blush instead of cream. It goes on easily and quickly with less unevenness of color. Have one light pink powder blush for the boys and a darker shade for the girls. Applying it with a three-inch powder puff is easier and quicker than using the regular brush applicator.

Use two shades of lipstick, a light pink for the boys and a darker shade for the girls. Avoid bright red or plum because they are too overpowering on children. Provide at least two tubes of lipstick for the boys and two for the girls, and make sure they are labeled. You will not use a whole tube of lipstick per show, but the stage manager always keeps one of each shade in her apron pocket during performances. Some children lick off their lipstick during the show, and the stage manager makes repairs. In one show, our entire cast seemed to be "lickers," keeping the stage manager busy throughout the play. If the thought of one tube of lipstick being applied to 30 mouths makes some germ-conscious mother squeamish or if a child has a known infection, that child may purchase a lipstick for his or her own use.

Eye shadow for boys is beige or brown. For girls use blue or green to coordinate with their costumes. Apply eyeliner to the upper lid only. Children's eyes tend to water when liner is applied to the lower lids. Use eyebrow pencil on children with light or scanty brows.

Except for redheaded children, we do not use mascara. It takes too much time to apply, and the children frequently smudge it before it is dry. Also, many children seem to be allergic to mascara, and red, swollen, itching eyes you can do without! Most redheads do need mascara because their eyelashes are so light that they are invisible to the audience.

Specialty Makeup

Because the makeup committee is busy with most of the children, I am usually responsible for specialty makeup. Once in a while we use dark pancake makeup. The beautiful girl who played Chief Sitting Bull in our *Annie Get Your Gun* needed a darker skin tone. We purchased pancake makeup in an "Egyptian" shade. We applied it with a wet sponge, covering her face, ears, neck and hands. She wore a long-sleeved shirt, so her arms were not exposed. As soon as the makeup dried, she dressed in her costume with a huge feathered headdress and was transformed into a very believable Indian chief.

We had special makeup needs for two characters in *The Wizard of Oz*. In order to dramatize the nastiness of the Wicked Witch of the West, we gave her a green face. Also, our Tin Woodman, with his bright silver costume, needed a silver face. Here was another case of "plan ahead." At Halloween time I was able to purchase face paint in both green and silver. I bought several tubes of each because I didn't know how much I needed and knew that no one would be selling it when April rolled around. The effect of the colored faces was superb, though it took practice to put the green on evenly.

Perhaps the trickiest problem we ever had was how to make our Anglo-Saxon children look Oriental for *The King and I*. None of the products we tried achieved the almond-eyed look we hoped for. Finally we settled for changing the shape of the eyebrows. Instead of eyebrows that dropped down at the outer edges, we wanted ours to go up slightly. We covered the children's eyebrows from the center point to the outer edges with a product intended to cover facial blemishes. Then we drew on new eyebrows with black grease pencils purchased from a theatrical supply store that we located through the Yellow Pages of the phone book. The result: children who looked more Oriental than before. Keep trying different applications until you achieve the look you desire.

Always try your makeup out on four or more children with the stage lights *before* dress rehearsal. (You'd be surprised at how many boys *volunteer* for this!) Makeup that looks fine in the daylight may be too pale under the stage lights. You may discover that the lipstick or rouge shade you had thought perfect is all wrong. You may have to adjust powder shades for some children or omit it altogether, as previously mentioned. Have all of these details worked out before you instruct your parent volunteers who will make up the entire cast. Be

The Cowardly Lion in *The Wizard of Oz* with his furry costume and whiskers was a favorite with the audience.

sure to use makeup at all dress rehearsals so that things will run smoothly at the student performance. Parents must practice too.

In *The King and I* we had one problem that was never solved, and we just had to live with it. That year many of our children, and especially those who played royal children, were blond. I purchased a bottle of nonpermanent hair color in black. One parent *volunteered* to try it on her child. If it worked, I planned to give the parents the option of using the product if they chose to do so. I sent the hair color home with the child whose mother had volunteered to try it. The report I got back the next day was, "It doesn't work. I tried five different times. As fast as I poured it on her head, it rolled right off again." Apparently a child's hair is so nonporous that it won't hold the color. So, we just had to settle for Siamese children with blond hair!

Makeup Stations

When the day of your first dress rehearsal arrives, you should set up the makeup area at least 1½ hours before performance time. Children dress in their costumes first and then report to the makeup table. Makeup is applied by an assembly-line system. Lay out supplies on a large table, forming six stations, three on each side of the table. Children will line up at one corner of the table and proceed around it from one station to the next. In the center of the table place a big box of facial tissues and several large bath towels to be wrapped around the children's shoulders to keep the powder off their costumes. A large paper bag goes under the table for trash.

Station no. 1 will be powder. As soon as the adult at that station has patted the powder onto their faces, the children proceed to station no. 2, which is rouge. Station no. 3 is lipstick, no. 4 eye shadow and no. 5 eyeliner (and mascara for redheads). Stations no. 3 and 5 should have two adults experienced with makeup assigned to them if possible because lipstick and eyeliner take longer to apply.

Station no. 6 is for hair. Supply that station with two hairbrushes, a comb, bobby pins in black and brown, hairpins, rubber bands and hair spray. This station is for ordinary hair-brushing needs. Assign someone away from the table to handle special hair jobs. Girls with long hair who play boys' parts will need extra help putting up their hair. Using this system, you should be able to put makeup on 35 faces in 45 minutes. Even 45 faces take only an hour. If you have more children, adjust your time schedule accordingly or set up a second table with the same stations.

Approximately one hour before the performance, parent makeup volunteers should arrive and be given their instructions. Be *sure* to tell the "lipstick" parents to *dab* on the lipstick and to see that the children *blot* their lipstick on a tissue.

The soloists and all others in the cast arrive for costuming at the same time the parents arrive. While the children are getting into their costumes, you have time to give the parents their instructions. As soon as the children finish dressing, they immediately report to the makeup table. Soloists are permitted to go to the head of the line so that they can finish quickly and then report to the musical director, who will warm up their voices. Fifteen minutes before performance time, the entire cast reports to the director for a last minute pep talk.

On the night of the last performance, things go quite smoothly. The children already know the routine, and they are usually ready, in costume and makeup, early. It has therefore become a tradition that I read them a special story, which takes about 15 minutes. The story is "The Bear Story," by James Whitcomb Riley. It is written in dialect, so I have practiced beforehand. I really throw myself into the story, pretending to cry when the boy in the story cries, etc. The children love the fact that their teacher-director is acting out the story and not afraid to appear foolish to them. Of course, I have an ulterior motive for doing this. In addition to using up extra time, I've totally distracted them, helping to calm nerves in a big way. Years later children have mentioned to me how much they'd loved "The Bear Story."

At last it's five minutes before the performance, and the cast walks to the stage. Right on time the show begins! Excitement! Applause! Pride!

10

Scenery

Good scenery adds special flair to your show. It fills the stage with color to create a mood. It makes the fantasy created by the actors more believable. The paint-by-number system we use combines adult planning and preparation with children's painting skills and enthusiasm. The result is beautiful and professional-looking scenery. Give it a try and the results will be amazing. Your youngsters will proudly boast to their families and friends that "I painted that!"

While you are choosing the script and modifying it for your youngsters during the summer months, consider the scenery needs along with all of the other aspects of the play. In fact, scenery requirements may determine whether you will be able to produce a particular play. A show requiring many elaborate and drastically different sets may be impossible to manage due to physical or economic limitations. If you really have your heart set on such a show though, consider whether all of the different sets are vital to the story line. Sometimes certain sets can be omitted and the action moved to a central area without affecting the plot. Try to limit sets to two or three main ones at most. Remember that changing scenery takes time. Too many changes slow the pace and break the flow of the show. A little judicious simplification may solve the problems.

If you already have a scenery designer discuss ideas and options with that person. Two heads are always better than one in working out thorny challenges. Consider the facilities on which you will present your play. Some groups are lucky enough to have a real stage with a full range of built-in features, such as curtains and lights. Other groups have no formal stage at all. Whatever your situation, there are a great many ways to enhance the facilities you do have. Things to check out are:

➤ What is the size of the stage area?

➤ How big an audience can be accommodated?

➤ Does the stage have front, back and side curtains?

➤ If there is a front curtain, is there sufficient space for short scenes to take place in front of it?

➤ Is there space backstage for actors and scenery between scenes?

➤ Are microphones available in the ceiling, on stands or on the floor?

➤ Are overhead lights, spotlights and footlights available?

➤ Can a backdrop or other scenery items be hung on the curtain or wall at the back of the stage? From the ceiling?

➤ Can flats and other scenery be easily carried on and off the stage?

➤ Where will the piano be placed?

Once you know both the good features and the limitations of your stage, it is time to consider the requirements of the play you have chosen. Some questions to ask are:

➤ Does most of the action happen indoors or outdoors? Can the story be simplified to occur mainly in one or the other?

➤ If some action occurs indoors, does it occur in distinctly different rooms? Does each room have a common characteristic?

➤ If some action occurs outdoors, is it in more than one geographic location?

➤ Does the passage of time need to be represented (e.g., seasonal changes such as leaf colors or clock movement)?

➤ Does action occur in a vehicle, such as a train, streetcar, stagecoach, or boat?

➤ What building exteriors are needed?

In our production of *The Music Man* most of the story took place in a town square. However, two scenes were supposed to happen in the local high school gymnasium. After wrestling with the question of how to create a gymnasium, I suddenly realized that the location of those two scenes had absolutely nothing to do with the story. We played the scenes in the town square, and they worked perfectly!

Scenery for Kids

Following the parents' meeting in October and the return of the parent sign-up forms, you hope to have a scenery designer and committee. You and the designer will begin to work out precisely what will be created and how. As with each phase of this project, the scenery must be designed and made with children in mind. In addition to suiting your stage and your show, it must be:

➤ Lightweight, safe and durable enough to be handled by stage crew children.
➤ Economical to make or purchase.
➤ Repairable, because accidents do happen.
➤ Easy to put up and take down.
➤ Easily transported, if you plan to take your show to other locations.

Check the library for books about Broadway shows and other plays. Many publications include photographs and illustrations for specific shows and are a rich source of ideas. Theater craft books are helpful. They are filled with ideas for marvelous sets including everything from a few cleverly placed lights to huge motorized sets elaborately depicting riverboats, trains or mountains. Obviously, such sophisticated sets are not for your children, but they can provide ideas that you may be able to adapt to meet your needs. If your show has been made into a movie, try to rent the video. Remember, good scenery enhances the show but never competes with the actors for attention.

Before rehearsals begin, you and the scenery designer should have a clear idea of what each scene will require and how to achieve it. Try to schedule Scenery Painting Day at least six weeks before the show if possible so that things do not become too rushed later when rehearsals are drawing to a busy conclusion. Of course, you will keep in touch with the scenery designer as well as the other chairmen, to keep preparations on schedule and in case they need help of any kind.

Designing the Scenery

In designing the scenery, consider using a backdrop and/or flats. A backdrop is a huge sheet of paper or other material, covering the back wall or back curtain of the stage, painted with the central scene. A backdrop is essential for stages with no rear curtains. Our earliest shows were performed on a fold-up stage in the school cafeteria. The backdrop covered the cinder block and tile wall behind the stage.

A flat is a free-standing wooden frame, covered with paper or material painted to depict whatever structures or other elements the scene requires. Our flats generally measure 3 × 6 feet and are reversible. By using them in a mix-and-match technique either with or without the backdrop, we are able to create many different scenes.

A backdrop alone was used in our production of *The King and I*, where 90 percent of the story took place in a royal palace. The interior of the palace was painted onto the backdrop in shades of purple, lavender and gold. The only other scene, on the deck of a boat, was created by lowering the lights on the backdrop and grouping a few barrels and baskets near the front of the stage where the action took place.

In *Annie* we were able to create three distinctively different scenes using six reversible flats and no backdrop. The opening scene inside a run-down orphanage used three flats depicting two broken windows and a door placed against our beige stage curtains. A laundry cart, table and chairs completed the scene. Three more flats were used for the next scene depicting a city street. On them the city skyline was painted in silhouette against a pale sky with a broken wooden slat fence in front. A shack was made from a refrigerator-shipping carton, and garbage cans were added for flavor. The final scene, inside a millionaire's mansion, used five flats placed across the back of the stage. The center flat showed a grand fireplace decorated with a Christmas wreath. The two flats on either side of the fireplace had huge Christmas trees decorated with glitter and metallic paper. The two outside flats were painted with floor-to-ceiling windows with heavy drapes and holiday garlands. Chandeliers of painted cardboard hung from the ceiling of the stage to complete the feeling of wealth.

Another production of *Annie* used a backdrop and three flats, relying heavily on color coordination to create both outdoor and indoor scenes. Silhouettes were strategically placed on the backdrop for outdoor scenes and were later covered by the flats to totally change the appearance for indoor scenes. Under a pale yellow sky, the New York City skyline was painted in charcoal gray with silhouetted skyscrapers pushing up in three evenly spaced places on the backdrop. For the indoor scenes, the pale yellow sky became pale yellow walls as flats were placed in front of the skyscrapers to depict interior windows and doors. The flats incorporated similar yellow tones. Scene changes were accomplished quickly.

For *Oklahoma!* we combined a backdrop and one flat. Most of the action happened outdoors so our backdrop was a rural landscape.

We used one reversible flat, which had a little house painted on one side and a barn on the other. By using the backdrop alone and in combination with the two sides of the flat, we created three different scenes.

These are just a few ideas for combining large scenery pieces. Many scenes can be supplemented with furniture, plants, fences, and hundreds of other items either made from cardboard or supplied by members of the community. We've made believable campfires by nailing logs to a plywood base and spraying them with neon orange paint to represent embers.

Simple but strong wooden boxes are invaluable for a multitude of purposes. They can be decorated to fit the scene, and the actors can stand or sit on them as needed. Play action at different levels is more visually interesting than at a single height. The boxes can be decorated to fit into many situations by covering them with paint, fabric or paper. Covered with satin, one of our boxes became a platform for the king in *The King and I*. Painted black, the boxes became seats for the witches in *The Wizard of Oz*. They can even be covered with wire and papier-mâché and painted to resemble rocks. Between shows, they can be used to store props backstage. For details see chapter 11, Backstage Dynamics, page 163.

Backdrop

A paper backdrop can be made in such a way that it fulfills all the requirements of student scenery. It can be made from readily available, fairly economical materials. It is lightweight and can be safely hung at the rear of the stage. It is easily painted by children in a paint-by-number format. It can be rolled up for storage or transportation in either a station wagon or van. It can be mended with paper or cloth tape. Perfect!

Once you have decided what your backdrop will look like, the next step is to measure the area to be covered by it. On a curtained stage, the paper backdrop can be pinned easily to the rear curtain using macramé T-pins. Be sure to measure the width of the rear of the stage. Some stages are trapezoid in shape, narrower at the rear than at the front. If you measure only the stage front and cut your backdrop accordingly, you may discover that it is too wide when the time comes to hang the backdrop. The year this happened to me, the backdrop was about two feet too wide on either side, so it wrapped around the corners. This effectively closed off the rear curtain openings and made it impossible for our young actors to use those areas for entrances and exits.

If you perform on a portable, folding stage such as those used in many school cafeterias, the backdrop should be the same width or a little wider than the stage. When deciding on placement of the stage, take into consideration the space you need for seating the audience and cast, storage of props, room for costume changes and such. You may be able to create "wings" to hide some backstage activities by using screens on either side of the stage. Conveniently located closets or hallways nearby may also serve as dressing rooms.

Once you have made a decision on stage placement, examine

Stage arrangement.

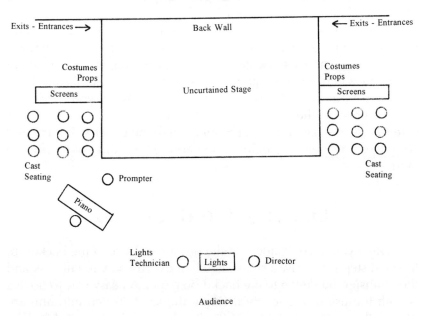

the wall behind the stage. If it is covered with cork or other bulletin board–type material, it will be easy to tack or staple the backdrop to the wall. If the wall is cinder block, you may need to attach a line of 1 × 3-inch furring strips to the wall. The backdrop can then be tacked or stapled to the wooden strip. Using masonry nails, attach the strip to the wall nine feet above the level of the stage floor, or whatever height you expect your backdrop to be.

Paper for the backdrop should be opaque, of medium-heavy

weight so that it will be durable and withstand frequent handling. Paint should not be able to soak through it, and it should not buckle too much when painted. In most cases white is the best color choice.

If you have a small budget, the best paper to buy for the backdrop is background paper sold at photographic supply stores. It is used by professional photographers as background material. It is available in nine-foot widths by 35-foot lengths in white and several other colors. It has a nice weight but tends to be slightly soft and easily torn at the edges. Therefore, your first task as soon as the paper is out of the box and cut to size is to reinforce the edges by applying two-inch masking tape all the way around on the back. In fact, two rows of tape at the bottom and top and three rows on either side are even better. The tape helps the paper resist curling after painting and makes the edges strong enough to withstand youngsters tripping over them as they paint.

If you are not able to purchase background paper but are committed to having a backdrop, consider whatever supplies you have at hand. Many schools stock large rolls of heavy paper measuring 36 inches in width for their students' art projects. Assembling a large backdrop from 36-inch strips is a tedious job, but if your budget is nonexistent and the paper is free, it can be done satisfactorily. Be sure to tape the paper before painting while the paper is still flat and the edges are even. The paint, when applied, should not loosen the tape.

Drawing the Backdrop

Once you have decided on the design and size of the backdrop, the next step is to draw a small sketch of exactly how it will look and then transfer the sketch to the backdrop paper. An easy way to do this is with the use of a grid. By dividing the small sketch into uniform blocks, the design can be transferred to the backdrop easily, block by block. If you have never tried this method, you will be pleased to discover what a labor-saving device a grid can be.

Begin the process with a small sketch, drawn to scale, with one inch equal to one foot of the finished backdrop. For example, if your backdrop is nine feet high by twenty-one feet long, the small sketch should be nine inches by twenty-one inches. On white paper using a medium-width black pen, draw a rectangle in the appropriate size, and then complete the grid by drawing vertical and horizontal lines spaced one inch apart. It will look like a checkerboard. Number each vertical line, top to bottom, and each horizontal line, left to right.

Over the grid, sketch the backdrop design with a pencil. The inked grid will endure many erasures and will simplify the job of sketching by providing handy horizontal and vertical lines, reducing the chore of measuring.

Grid and scenery sketch.

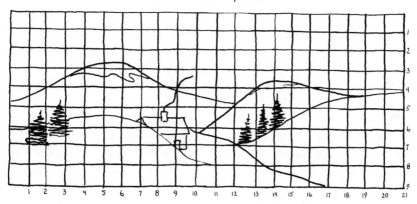

As you are designing, keep in mind that the scenery should be scaled to the height of the children in the cast. Buildings, doorways, fences, etc. should appear to be sized as though the actors were adults. If the average height of your cast is four feet, then ordinary doorways should be at least that height. If your stage is very deep and the eye level of the audience is low, doorways and other structures may appear lower than they actually are. Also, the short curtains, called teasers, hanging from the ceiling of a curtained stage may hide the top few inches of the backdrop.

If the backdrop calls for a landscape or architectural detail with which you are unfamiliar, check with the local library for a book on the subject. The children, caught up in the play and its background, will be studying the geography, culture and history of the location or time period of the play. The accuracy of the scenery will reinforce what they are learning.

In addition, the library is full of simple how-to art books. A quick study of perspective may be helpful if you have never before thought about horizons or vanishing points. This is the old railroad-track-into-the-sunset principle, which demonstrates that parallel lines converge as they go away from the eye. Another hint: An outdoor scene is more artistically pleasing if the horizon line, the point where the sky meets the earth, is not in the precise center between the top and bottom of the backdrop. As helpful as art books may be, don't be frightened by the rules. If talk of perspective intimidates you, just stay away from complicated angles and plan a simple backdrop that avoids all those problems. If you like the way something looks, even if it does not do exactly what the books say it should, use it anyway.

The best piece of advice I can give you about your scenery design is *keep it simple*. Avoid a lot of fussy details. They will not be visible to the audience anyway and will complicate the children's painting job. Scenery is intended to create an impression and to enhance the acting by providing an attractive and complementary background. The backdrop should not be so distracting that it jars the audience's attention away from the most important thing on the stage—the children!

The payoff for the scenery designer is a chance to have some fun and let the imagination soar. Here is the chance to create something huge, beautiful and impressive. Just think how many artists would love to have 189 square feet of their work on public display!

Once the design is finished, transfer it to the backdrop paper by following the grid, block by block. If you do not have enough space to lay the backdrop paper out completely, the grid can easily be worked in sections, rolling and unrolling the paper from one side to the other. The first step is to grid the backdrop paper with a pencil in the same manner as your one-inch grid, using one-foot blocks instead. Number the horizontal and vertical lines as you did the smaller grid. Complicated designs require a complete grid. Later as you become more experienced, you may be able to eliminate some areas of the grid. An example would be backdrops that include vast areas of sky. In the beginning, it is best to play it safe and draw the entire grid. A reasonably straight six-foot furring strip makes a great drawing aid. Measure off one-foot segments at the top and bottom of the paper. Then line up the furring strip between the pairs of marks, and draw a line along its edge.

Next you will draw the design onto the backdrop paper. The grid will make it easy. Using a pencil, draw the design one block at a time, matching the larger version to the smaller. For example, if a line of the small version in block #1 goes from the lower left corner of the square to the upper right corner, simply draw it that way on the larger version. Yardsticks, T squares, angles and other drawing tools are handy if you have them. If you don't, your house is full of other items that work well. Art supply stores sell a compass that slips over a yard-stick for drawing circles up to two yards in diameter. The same thing can be accomplished cheaply by tying a string to a pencil and holding the free end of the string to the paper with the thumb while swinging the pencil in an arc. Smaller circles can be drawn easily using household items such as tape rolls, dishes, even lamp shades as patterns. Special shapes, such as the points of a wrought iron fence or gingerbread trim of a house, can be duplicated consistently by making a cardboard pattern and tracing around it.

Transferring the design

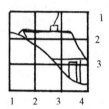

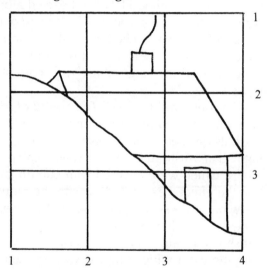

If you make a mistake and erase it, try to brush away the eraser dust because grit under the paper can puncture the paper as you kneel on it to draw. Speaking of knees, garden knee pads reduce the stress of kneeling on a hard floor for a long time.

This part of the job is the greatest fun. It is exciting to see your design begin to take shape. Once the design is completely drawn, use a black felt-tipped marker to highlight the lines of the man-made structures. Use appropriately colored markers to outline natural objects such as trees, mountains, etc. When painted, these lines may not be fully covered by paint. When finished, the backdrop will resemble a large page from a child's coloring book.

The Flat

The chances are that you will want more than just a single backdrop for your show. Lightweight flats are versatile and fairly easy to make. A flat is a freestanding wooden frame to which is attached the same kind of paper used for the backdrop, painted in the desired design. Our first flats measured four feet wide by six feet high. They were covered with paper left over from the backdrop. Later flats measured three feet wide by six feet high so that we could use 36-inch paper available in the school art supplies cabinet.

Flats can be one-sided or reversible. They can be made to look like almost anything. Flats can be used alone, grouped or in combination with the backdrop. In *The Wizard of Oz* our flat was Dorothy's house. After it was picked up by the cyclone and dropped in Oz, we attached a rainbow to it. In *Oklahoma!* we grouped three flats on either side of the stage, three with corn stalks and three with sunflowers.

For one production of *The Sound of Music* we had a 4 × 6-foot flat with hinged wings measuring two feet each in width. For the opening hillside scene, the wings were folded back out of sight, and the flat had an Austrian mountain scene. Later in the Von Trapp home the wings, which were covered with curtain fabric, were opened out so that the effect was a window with the mountain view beyond. Later the wings were swung shut and the flat reversed, creating the appearance of a window with the curtains pulled. The opposite side of the flat showed stained glass windows and was used in the abbey. Even with the extra wings, the flat was light enough for the young stage crew to manage. (See page 141.)

If you decide to build a flat, start out by thinking about size and weight.

➤ It must balance well, and the stage crew must be able to lift it easily.
➤ It must fit on your stage along with the actors, dancers, etc.
➤ If you are invited to perform somewhere and have to transport it, it must fit into your vehicle.
➤ It must move easily through doorways.
➤ The paper you have must fit it.

Next find someone who can make the flats. You don't need a professional cabinetmaker. A flat is not fine furniture and will be covered

Sketch of *Sound of Music* set

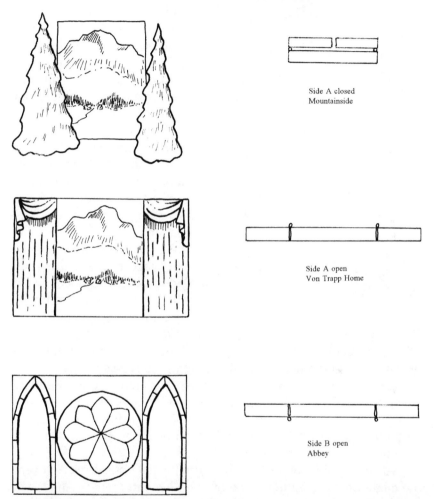

Side A closed
Mountainside

Side A open
Von Trapp Home

Side B open
Abbey

by paper anyway. It does, however, have to be sturdy, stand straight, and balance itself. There is bound to be at least one do-it-yourself carpenter in the neighborhood who will take pity on you and lend a hand.

A simple rectangular frame built with 1 × 3 × 72-inch furring strips will do nicely. A strip across the middle will strengthen the frame and make it less likely to warp. The strips are wide enough to allow the paper to be stapled on easily. Purchased or donated lumber that is as straight as possible will yield the best result.

One way to join the pieces is with a splice plate or nailer plate

Flat, 4 × 6 feet, showing nailer plates and 6 × 21-inch footings, with metal angle

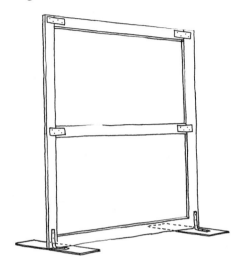

available at most hardware stores. It is a flat piece of metal with small holes. It is laid over the two pieces of wood to be joined and nails are driven through the holes. Your carpenter may have other good ideas.

The feet that hold the flat upright are two 6 × 21-inch pieces of plywood or rigid metal. They are attached to the flat on either side by screwing metal angles to the flat and the feet. The feet may be painted the same color as the stage to make them less noticeable. The side edges of the flat can be painted black or another neutral color.

If the flat has a tendency to bounce during a dance number or otherwise seems unstable, place something heavy on each foot, out of sight behind the flat. A bag filled with sand works well.

Once the flats are made, cut paper to fit them and reinforce the back edges with masking tape in the same manner as the backdrop. Design the flat and transfer the design using a grid. These sheets will be painted along with the backdrop on Scenery Painting Day and then stapled to the flats.

At some point you may wish to turn the flat on its side. An example might be the opening scene of *The King and I* where Anna is on the ship arriving in Bangkok. The flat might be painted to look like a ship's railing with cleats, ropes, barrels, etc. Of course, the flat will not look like a complete ship, so for this scene, darken the stage and spotlight the flat, which is placed near the front, particularly if the scene involves only one or two characters. Depending on the type and vintage of the ship in the scene, props such as fishing nets, sea chests, anchors and sails could be used to soften the edges of the flat by arranging the props in order of decreasing height and fading into the darkness at the edges of the spotlighted area. (See page 143.)

A "ship" using flat and props

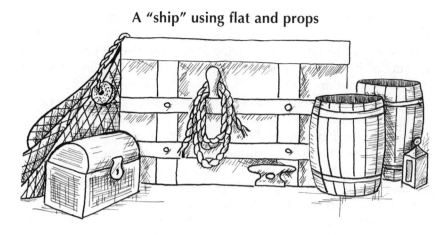

Choosing Colors

You have probably been thinking all along about the colors you might want to use in the scenery, but now is the time to make the final choices. Consider not only the impression made by the color of the backdrop but also the color's interaction with the stage lights, costumes and props.

The scenery designer and costume coordinator may need to devise a harmonious color scheme together. The colors must work together, drawing the eye into the scene and leading it naturally to the action of the play. In our production of *The Wizard of Oz* we deliberately planned to keep color out of the opening scene in Kansas, letting the neutral beige stage curtains do the job. Once Dorothy had landed in the Land of Oz, we used vibrant neon colors in both costumes and scenery to show that Dorothy was definitely not in Kansas anymore.

We live with color all our lives, but how many people really think about the effect it has on them? Warm colors, such as red and orange, send a message of happiness, excitement and action. Visually, they advance toward the audience's eye. Cooler colors, blues and greens, seem to recede from the audience and have a lazy, calming effect. Use this knowledge to create the right mood for your show.

You will be creating a paint-by-number picture for your child-painters. Most schools stock nontoxic water-based tempera paint in basic colors for students' use. It is economical and safe for children. Tempera paint has a couple of disadvantages when used for scenery. It tends to flake off the paper if applied too thickly at full strength, particularly if the paper is rolled. Your backdrop will almost certainly have to be rolled up since few schools or homes have enough room to leave a 9 × 21-foot backdrop lying about. The flaking problem can be reduced by thinning the paint with water and asking the children to apply it in a thin, even coat.

The second annoying characteristic is that results are sometimes unpredictable when mixing two primary colors. The primary colors are red, yellow and blue as shown on the color wheel. Theoretically, you should be able to mix any other color from those three. However, mixing clear blue tempera with clear yellow tempera does not necessarily result in the expected lovely green. Sometimes it just turns to mud. This quirk seems to be related to the chemistry of the paint. You will just have to experiment with different combinations of colors to find the one you want. Keep track of the proportions, rather like a recipe, and after making up several samples, choose the one that seems best for your purposes.

Color wheel

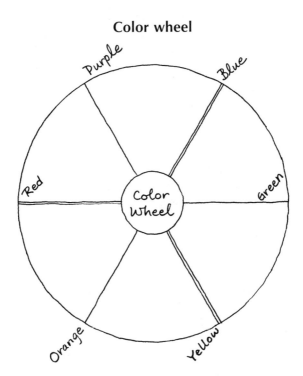

After mixing up a few paint samples, try them out on a small rough sketch of your scenery to be sure the colors work well together.

Generally, full-strength, undiluted paint colors are too intense for the backdrop. In addition to flaking, they will fight with the costumes for attention. Tone them down by adding water or white tempera for a more pastel shade, or add a touch of the color opposite it on the color wheel to achieve a grayed tone. For example, to subdue red, add green, which is a mixture of blue and yellow, the colors opposite red on the wheel. Also, keep in mind the effect the stage lights will have on the colors.

Related colors near each other on the color wheel, such as purple and blue, can be used together in large quantities. Sometimes a monochromatic color scheme, using shades of a single color such as yellow, gold and brown, can be done in a striking fashion. Contrasting colors are those opposite each other on the color wheel, such as red and green. Using large and nearly equal areas of contrasting colors is seldom pleasing to the eye. Save the strong colors and contrasts for highlights and costumes.

As you mix the paint and decide which to use for the scenery, make a paint color chart by numbering a sheet of paper and putting a dab of paint next to each number. These numbers will correspond to numbers you will place on the backdrop to guide the student painters. Our backdrops have had from 12 to 30 different shades of paint and the children have handled them well. As you work you may find that some colors change too much when they dry. You can speed the process by drying the dabs with a hair dryer to see the true color.

Once the colors are chosen, go back to the backdrop and build the paint-by-number scheme by numbering each area to correspond to the paint chart. Use a red pencil for the paint colors so that the children will not be confused by other numbers and markings you may have used during measuring and sketching. Red pencil marks stand out but are easily covered, even by light paint colors.

Scenery Painting Day

It is almost time for your young painters to get into the act. Schedule Scenery Painting Day about six weeks before the performance. You will need a room large enough to spread out the backdrop and other scenery and have room left over for the children to walk around it. The cafeteria is a good choice, but a classroom can be used if the desks are removed. It will take approximately two hours for 24 children to do all the painting. Remind the children to wear their old clothes that day, although tempera paint is washable.

Call the adults who have volunteered to help to tell them that Scenery Painting Day has been scheduled. Friday is our favorite day for scenery painting because the backdrop can dry thoroughly over the weekend before the paper is rolled up. Mix the paint a day or two ahead. If you do this too far ahead, the paint may become moldy or the can may rust and stain the paint.

Each paint color is mixed according to the color chart and placed in an empty one-pound coffee can with a tight plastic lid. If you remember to ask the parents to collect coffee cans at the time of the parent meeting, you should have plenty by this time. Offices are a good source of coffee cans. One-pound coffee cans are ideal for this purpose. They are a size that is easy for youngsters to handle, and those tight plastic lids keep the paint from drying out. Attach a piece of masking tape to the side of the can and write the paint number on the tape and lid with a felt-tipped marker. Keep the number of painters in mind as you mix the paint. You want to have as many children as possible painting simultaneously, so mix several cans of those colors that cover large areas. In fact, for large quantities of certain colors such as sky blue, I like to mix the paint in a large plastic bucket and then pour it into several labeled coffee cans. Be sure to bring some empty cans with blank labels for Scenery Painting Day. Situations often arise in which two painters are more efficient if each has her own can of paint. Just pour a little of the original supply into a spare can. Be sure to label that can right away. Some shades are so similar that they are difficult to identify later.

Scenery Painting Day will be easier if you remember to bring along a few basic survival supplies. Besides paper, paint, brushes and newspaper, you will need long-handled spoons, such as iced tea-spoons, to stir up the paint just before it is used. It settles quickly, some-times overnight. A roll of paper towels or a good supply of rags may be worth their weight in gold if one of your Rembrandts is butter-fingered. We've been lucky in this regard. Out of almost four hundred scenery painting children in sixteen years, we've had only one spill.

Pencils, masking tape, felt markers and big plastic garbage bags for trash also come in handy. Plastic buckets or tall cans, such as 46-ounce juice cans, are good for soaking dirty brushes. Don't leave the brushes standing on their bristles too long though or they may be ruined. Ordinary half-inch school art brushes are adequate for this job. We also have on hand some smaller brushes for detail work. We have tried having the children use old two-inch latex brushes for large areas of a single color. However, we find that the painters are not as precise using the bigger brushes.

On Scenery Painting Day, explain the paint-by-number system to the adult volunteers, and assign them their tasks of answering children's questions and cleaning brushes. Roll out the backdrop and other scenery, and ask a volunteer or student to put newspaper under the *edges* of the paper. It is usually not necessary to put newspaper under the entire piece. However, double-check to be certain the paint will not seep through the paper.

Spread several thicknesses of paper on a table and line up the cans of paint in a row with the numbers facing toward the children. Ask a volunteer to remove the lids. Stir up any paint that has settled. Locate a nearby sink and fill a bucket or tall cans with water, and assign an adult to be in charge of cleaning brushes.

It is best to do all this preparation before the children arrive on the scene. They will be excited and eager to plunge into the project. Enjoy their oohs and aahs as they marvel at your wonderful drawing. Hold them back for a few more minutes while you describe how they will turn this plain paper into beautiful scenery. Show them the sketches and color chart. Explain how a paint-by-number painting works. Tell them to stay inside the black marker lines and to ignore the pencil lines and numbers. Stress the importance of matching the numbers on the paint cans with the *red* numbers on the paper. Tell them that these few tips will make everything turn out fine:

➤ All children must remove their shoes so that the paper will not be torn.

➤ Begin painting in the middle of the paper and work toward the outside edges. Otherwise, you may kneel in wet paint.

➤ Watch out for your neighbor, his brush and his can of paint.

➤ Make sure the number on your can of paint matches the *red* number marked on the scenery.

➤ Apply the paint in an even, thin coat. Make sure it completely covers the paper, but avoid globs of paint.

➤ Brush in every direction (north, south, east and west). Avoid scrubbing the paper with the brush because it's easy to wear a hole in the paper.

➤ Rinse your brush thoroughly in water before you begin painting with a new color. The old color could muddy up the new one.

➤ When you are not sure about something, don't guess. *Ask!*

Working head-to-head, many children can paint the backdrop simultaneously with outstanding results.

It is critical that every child understand the directions. One year we had an especially large number of foreign-born student-painters who were studying English as a second language. We decided to assign each of them a partner who would listen to my directions in English and translate them into other languages. I said a sentence or two and then waited while our translators did their job. After a couple of cycles I noticed one translator who was giving the directions to his partner, very precisely, very slowly, and very loudly … in English. Happily, the painting went smoothly.

Assign each child an area near the center of the backdrop, and the group may begin painting. By having two rows of painters kneel head-to-head in the center of the backdrop with their feet toward the outside edges, as many as 25 children may paint a 9 × 21-foot backdrop simultaneously without problems. They will probably finish in under two hours. Especially skilled child-artists may be assigned intricate areas. The same system is used with flats and other smaller scenery pieces.

The paper may pucker a bit when it is wet, but most of the puckers will disappear as the paint dries. Those that remain will never be noticed by the audience.

The children who participate in Scenery Painting Day become totally and happily absorbed in the job of painting. Discipline is *never* a problem. All of the children are thrilled to have a part in the project, and they proudly show their share of the finished masterpiece to their friends. "That's my fence!" "Those are my flowers!" They adopt the scenery as their very own creation, and it truly is theirs. They become very protective of it, even standing guard over it to prevent other children from coming too close.

Make sure the paint is completely dry before you try to roll up the backdrop and other scenery. There is one more touch that sharpens the look of the scenery. Often during painting some paint will have slopped over the marker lines. The black lines seem to bring out the details of buildings, fences and other synthetic structures. So, your scenery designer may wish to freshen up those lines with a new black marker. Trees, flowers and other natural features are usually not outlined in black, unless you want a cartoon-like look. An especially brave and artistic scenery designer may even be willing to highlight, shade or texture the backdrop to give it a more three-dimensional, realistic look. This should be done with a very light touch, however, because the children will be offended if they think someone has changed their wonderful work of art.

To secure the backdrop to the wall or back curtain of your stage, use staples, tacks or macramé T-pins. They can be driven through the upper edge of the paper safely because it is well reinforced with masking tape. However, if you plan to take your show to other locations and the backdrop must be put up more than once, the pins may eventually wear holes in the paper. A little trick to avoid that problem is to devise tabs attached to the top of the backdrop. The tabs can be pinned or tacked, leaving the backdrop itself untouched. Use two-inch cloth-backed duct tape. Cut a piece approximately 12 inches long. Stick the lower six inches to the back of the top edge of the backdrop. Then fold over the remaining six inches on itself, forming a three-inch tab. Space the tabs across the top edge every 18 inches or so. We always use these tabs on our backdrops to avoid any damage to the children's work. (See page 150.)

Now the backdrop is ready whenever you need it. Roll it loosely and tie it with string for storage. If it must be carried outside on a rainy day, protect it from water spots by wrapping it in a painter's plastic drop cloth, 9 × 12 feet. You will probably hang the backdrop a couple of days before the first dress rehearsal. For safety's sake, this is a job for adults in most cases.

Backdrop tabs

Feet-in-Concrete Trick

We borrowed this trick from gangster novels, and it is a super way to support any small piece of scenery such as a bush, flag, tombstone, sign, mailbox or any other light object. The key is a 1-inch piece of wood or dowel, approximately three to four feet long, which is anchored in concrete in a three-pound coffee or shortening can. Pound three or four nails into the base of the dowel, and anchor it in ready-mix concrete in the can. The nails help to hold the dowel in the concrete. The ready-mix concrete is available at the hardware store, mixes with a garden hoe or trowel and hardens quickly. A 67-pound sack of mix will fill about ten cans. The concrete is heavy enough to support fairly large pieces of cardboard without tipping over on stage. Paint the cans and dowels with leftover paint. The cans become nearly invisible when painted to match the backdrop or curtain.

We used these cans for huge neon colored plants in the Land of Oz and for topiary trees in *Annie Get Your Gun*. We also used them to support windows in the train scene from that show. The supports could barely be detected against the red curtain.

Miniflats

Another handy item is a miniflat, which is simply a piece of cardboard, 2 × 6 feet, cut from a refrigerator carton or other large box. It can be painted to resemble a low fence, stone wall, hedge or even a small flower garden. It can change the look of a backdrop by covering some feature near the bottom. Nail the cardboard to a 2 × 2-inch board and attach 2 × 6-inch feet similar to those used in the flat for balance. The miniflat can be reversible too.

Top: **Canned concrete support and topiary tree.**
Bottom: **Miniflat as a stone wall, front and back.**

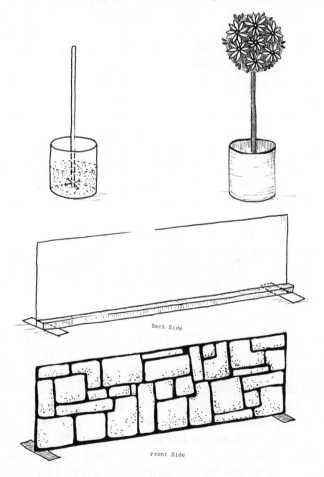

Trains

In addition to boats, your show may call for a train or streetcar scene. Both *Annie Get Your Gun* and *The Music Man* had train scenes that we played either near the front of the stage or in front of a curtain, if available. A row of cardboard seats attached to chairs creates a convincing side view of a train car. The seats can be arranged either all facing in the same direction or facing each other in pairs, depending on the show. If a great deal of conversation between the characters takes place on the train, seats in pairs may look more natural than having all the young actors sit facing forward and twist in their seats to speak to each other. Either way, two chairs may be placed behind each cardboard front to make the illusion of a wide train seat.

Step one is to decide on the arrangement, type and number of chairs to be used in the scene. Generally, nonfolding chairs are best if available. Step two is to find some pieces of cardboard large enough to hide chairs viewed from the side. Furniture stores are likely sources for big boxes.

Make a pattern by placing the cardboard against the side of the chair and trace around the chair. Then design the shape of the seat, making it larger than the chair outline. You can build in fanciful shapes and curlicues to suggest plush cushions if you wish. Just be sure you don't build the arm and back of the chair up so high that when the actors sit normally in the chairs, they are hidden from the audience's view.

Cut out the cardboard seat using a razor blade cutter. The type used for trimming wallpaper is ideal. Buy a box of utility-grade razor blades because you will be using quite a few. Be sure to cut on top of a piece of scrap cardboard or plywood so that the razor blade does not damage your work surface.

All of the remaining seats can be drawn and cut by using the original as a pattern. Painting will be easier if you use the inside of the box, the side with no printing, toward the front. If you have decided to use the pairs-of-seats arrangement be sure to cut half of the seats facing right and half facing left.

Once that is done, figure out what pattern, if any, you want to have on the side of the seat. Your children may have some good ideas about this. Possibilities are the name of the train, a monogram, a floral or geometric shape. Draw the design onto ordinary typing paper and transfer it to each seat by sandwiching a piece of carbon paper between the design and the cardboard and tracing the design. Go over the design with a wide felt-tipped marker, and the seats can be painted with tempera on Scenery Painting Day by the children.

Some cardboard has a tendency to curl toward the painted side. We've tried two different solutions that seem to work equally well.

Train seats

1. Trace outline of chair onto cardboard.

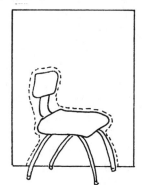

2. Draw and cut shape of train seat.

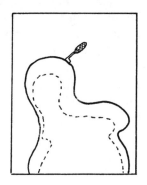

3. Trace design onto seat using carbon paper.

4. Tape train seat back to chair.

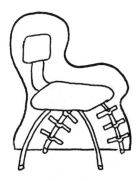

One is to place a heavy object such as a can of paint in the center of the seat to hold it flat while it dries. The other is to paint the back of the cardboard so that the curling of the two sides cancel each other out. Using that method, I usually prepare the cardboard back before the children paint the fancy front.

To attach the seats to the chairs, use masking tape. Use several long strips on each chair leg so that the cardboard is securely held to the side of the chair. Make sure you use enough tape so that the seat front can withstand a small amount of bumping without loosening. As the actors move in and out of the seats, they may accidentally bump the seat front, and the audience may be treated to the amusing sight of the chair front falling flat on the stage.

If you plan to perform your show at several locations and use chairs available at each site, the repeated application and removal of masking tape may begin to tear away the top layers of cardboard on the back of the seat. One solution is to apply long strips of cloth-backed duct tape along the areas where the masking tape will be applied. The masking tape will stick easily to the duct tape and can be removed without tearing the duct tape or cardboard. During the performance, keep extra masking tape on hand for quick repairs between scenes. Make sure your stage crew has many opportunities to practice carrying the train seats on and off the stage so they can learn how to do so without bending or tearing the seat fronts.

Children are fiercely proud and protective of three things: their play, their costumes and their scenery. With the scenery you have added an entirely new dimension to their play, and they realize how hard you have worked to help them make their play one of the best things they've ever done. You've become their special friend, and a child's friendship is a joyous gift.

11

Backstage Dynamics

Backstage is the unglamorous but vital side of play production. If the audience is to enjoy a flawless performance on stage, things must run smoothly backstage. It is truly the testing ground for all the planning and rehearsing that has gone on before. Although most of the props and scenery are handled by the stage crew children, there must be adults backstage to maintain order, handle emergencies, control stage and house lights, pull the curtain and other responsibilities beyond the capabilities of young children. They must also give the children important moral support during the performance.

Stage Manager

The stage manager is the backstage counterpart to the director and has the ultimate responsibility for everything that goes on backstage. If this job sounds as appealing as playing the underdog in a Christians vs. lions confrontation, don't be fooled. The job of stage manager is exciting and rewarding work. Nothing can match seeing the glow on the children's faces when they hear the applause for the first time and hearing the marvelous things they say about the experience they are having. One boy in total amazement said, "Gee, they *love* us!"

A teacher makes an ideal stage manager because she knows how to handle children and the children already accept her as an authority figure. Lacking that, you must find a parent who has an iron hand and a heart of gold. By opening night she must know the play well and be a familiar face to the children, so she must be willing to attend the final month of rehearsals and all performances. (We have always used an at-home parent because of the considerable time demands of this job.) Assisting her should be an adult on the opposite side of the stage. It is best if this person, too, is able to attend rehearsals for at least the month prior to the first performance.

Although the responsibilities of the stage manager are basically the same during rehearsal as they are during a performance, her approach to them is different. Our original stage manager, Anne, developed a philosophy from her backstage experiences, her common sense and her great human understanding. It made so much sense that her philosophy was followed by all those who succeeded her in that job. During rehearsal you must maintain an atmosphere of order, cooperation and hard work. Rehearsals can become tiring and boring, especially to children who must spend endless hours waiting backstage for their cues. Some ten-year-olds dream up ingenious ways to occupy themselves at such times. You must convince them that what they do offstage is just as important as what they do onstage. Talking and mischief are unprofessional and can ruin what is happening onstage. For some children a scowl followed by a smile is enough to bring them back into line. Others require more imaginative measures. Let them know that you will be hard on their behavior but not on them.

During the month of March those children with minor parts are allowed to sit out front and watch the rehearsal, with the condition that they *quietly* return backstage before their presence is required onstage. This always seems to work well, as they become caught up in the action of the play and forget to misbehave.

I usually have a short cast meeting lasting no more than a minute or two before each rehearsal, once we begin practicing on our real stage. At our very first meeting I lay down the rules: (1) no talking backstage; (2) no walking around backstage; (3) do not touch any prop unless you are picking it up to carry it onstage; (4) any misbehavior will be corrected only once, and after that the child will be sent home from that rehearsal in disgrace. *You must then stick to every rule you have made. If you overlook even one infraction, you are lost! The children will reason that you may overlook the next one, too.*

The entire cast must sit backstage at all times and must be very quiet and *not* move around, beginning with the first dress rehearsal. As mentioned before, once when all the adults backstage were busy with various jobs one child decided to stick a paper clip into an electrical outlet and blew out every fuse in the school! Why he wasn't killed, we'll *never* know!

During the actual performances, the atmosphere is totally different. The children will be nervous and scared, so let them know that you understand how they feel, that you are going to give them all the support you can and that you are expecting great things of them. Keep everything upbeat. Once the show starts, give a physical sign, such as thumbs-up, to show that everything is going to be OK. When they do something well, react as though you are as proud as they are. If they make a mistake, tell them it is all right. Use plenty of praise and only constructive criticism, such as "smile" or "louder." No negative criticism should be used on this occasion. If you have to make them stop talking, make a funny face so they get the message without feeling stepped on. Be certain that your assistants understand this gentle approach on this special day.

During all rehearsals, beginning in early January, Barbara, our assistant director, wrote on her script every single direction I gave to any child actor. Some examples are: (1) Max—sit with kids; (2) Philip—have whistle in hand; (3) Munchkins—back up and point; (4) Witch—get up, swish skirt, pat hair; (5) strobe off, lights on; (6) Marian—breathe here; (7) Harold—gesture with hands to indicate uniform. Before rehearsing a scene, she would remind each child of the directions that applied to that child. It wasn't long before those directions became second nature to the children.

As stage manager, Barbara needed a new script for dress rehearsals and performances because her markings were different. For instance, she might write (1) Curtain; (2) Darlene-mike-announcement; (3) House lights on; (4) Mikes off; (5) Spots off; (6) Footlights off; (7) Ten-minute intermission. Also, using different colored pens for different jobs, she notes changes in scenery, costumes, props and who is responsible for them, curtains, house and stage lights, microphone settings, and any of the other 1,001 details that every show has. If a particular job such as curtain closing must be done exactly on cue, she underlines the last line of the preceding song or dialogue to remind herself that a change is coming up. Make sure all backstage assistants have the same notations in their scripts, in case a task is to be done by someone else. Each assistant might color key all tasks that apply to him or her.

In addition to these reminders, the stage manager should work out a signal system with the director, who will be seated in the audience in her line of vision. They will decide whether an extra bow or encore is appropriate at the end of the show.

Tips for the Stage Manager

With your script in hand, *you, the stage manager,* are the backstage nerve center. You will find it convenient to have a cobbler's or carpenter's apron with lots of pockets. In it you will keep your script and pen plus all of the other repair equipment you might need on a moment's notice to deal with ripped costumes, smudged lipstick, mussed hair and all manner of catastrophes. Include boys' and girls' lipstick, hair brush, masking tape, safety and hair pins, Band-Aids, small scissors and three sewing needles threaded with white, black and another predominant color thread secured in a piece of cardboard. You may also wish to have on hand a few pieces of 12 × 12-inch cardboard and a felt-tipped marker to make signs to use for signaling the cast, such as "freeze," "encore," and other ad-libs as needed.

As stage manager you will be responsible for checking costumes before the show. If a child must change costume during the course of the show, and you have no way to move from one side of the backstage area to the other, it is imperative that his costume be on the side of the stage on which he exits in that scene. Note in your script a complete list of costumes for stage right and another list for stage left. Check and double-check them before each performance.

In *Annie,* Rooster quickly changed his looks by adding a mustache and suit coat.

Costumes that wrinkle easily will have to be hung on coat hangers. Coat hangers have a nasty habit of turning into a tangled mess when abandoned during a show and making an awful racket when accidentally dropped. Try to keep metal ones to a minimum; plastic hangers are less noisy when dropped. During the show, as the children stand ready to enter the stage, quickly glance at their attire to be certain the blouse is tucked in, the fly is zipped and the shoes are tied.

On opening night have a small jug of water and five-ounce paper cups handy for the soloists to have a sip of water when they exit after a number. The rest of the cast may have a sip during the intermission, but only a sip, because no one may leave the stage during a performance to go to the bathroom except in dire circumstances and only with the permission of the stage manager. I remember one child who had such an emergency when he exited the stage in the middle of a scene. He had to re-enter the stage later in the scene, so his trip to the bathroom was a speedy one. When he returned he heard his re-entrance cue line, and he hurried on stage. It wasn't long before everyone heard a few snickers from the audience; then there were more. I looked carefully at the child, and noticed that the end of his tie was peeking out of his zipped fly like a flag unfurled! There wasn't a single thing we could do about it but fix it when he exited the next time. Thank goodness the child was mature enough to laugh it off instead of becoming upset!

Stage Crew

When you cast your play in early December, you will choose a stage crew to be responsible for scenery and props during the show. The number chosen will be determined by the number of your sets and props, but four children have been adequate to handle the requirements of most of our shows. Scene changes should occur smoothly, quickly and quietly. Because a scene can be spoiled by the absence of an important prop, the stage crew should consist of reliable students, ones you can trust never to let you down. Assign certain scenery pieces and certain props to each child so each one knows his area of responsibility. Make a master list showing scenery and props for each scene. Print it on a large cardboard sheet in bold letters with a felt-tipped marker so it is easy to read backstage where it is often dark. Prop requirements for each scene are printed in color to distinguish them from scenery requirements which are printed in black. Each stage crew member has a different color on the chart, to mark the things in his area of responsibility. The master list used by the stage crew for *Annie* resembled the partial list below.

Master Scenery & Props List

Act 1	*Scene 2*
Scene 1	Hooverville flats
Orphanage-3 flats	Box w. paper hats
Mops	Fire, pot, ladle
Molly-doll	Apple Seller-apples
Annie-sweater, note	Artie-hammer
Bundles-laundry cart	Fred-magazine, cup

In Scene One of *Annie* each orphan had a pillow and shared a blanket with another orphan; the orphans rather than the stage crew were responsible for these.

Appoint one member of the crew to act as stage crew chief. Things seem to go better if one person has the final responsibility. It is his job to double check each detail before the scene opens. He must make sure that the right scenery is on stage, that the props are in the right hands and that all costume changes have been completed. He receives a nod from the stage manager, his fail-safe system, and then signals with a flashlight to the lights technician, who turns on the stage lights for the scene to begin.

When you begin rehearsals in January, emphasis will be on dialogue and staging, and you will use only absolutely necessary props. As rehearsals proceed through February, begin to introduce more props. The presence of the stage crew members at rehearsals is not required until early March. It doesn't take them three months to learn their jobs, especially with the use of the master scenery and props list. The part of their job that generates the most "grumbles" is putting everything away at the end of rehearsals. This includes flats and all props. Many of the props may be borrowed items, and their safekeeping is essential.

When the stage crew first attends rehearsals, there is no scenery attached to the flats. The children must get used to handling these large structures, bringing them on- and offstage without a spill. You might choose to staple a plain sheet of paper on each flat so that they can learn to handle them without sticking their fingers through the paper. If you used the painted version in rehearsal, it might suffer a fatal case of wear and tear before the first performance. The week of the first dress rehearsal is the best time to add the painted scenery.

If your stage has a curtain, it is possible to change sets while a scene takes place in front of the curtain. However, it must be done silently, particularly if the stage has overhead microphones, so that the scene going on out front is not spoiled by noise from behind the curtain. If you have an uncurtained stage, it is especially important that scene changes occur smoothly, since they happen on a darkened stage but still right before the eyes of the audience. Because they are visible to the audience, stage crew members who choose not to have acting parts should wear a simple costume appropriate to the show, even if it is only a vest, neckerchief or hat. This may seem a small detail, but it helps to maintain the mood of the show. In addition, it makes these children feel important to have their own costumes, just as the rest of the cast does.

Remember that your stage crew members are children, though reliable ones. They need to practice their jobs just as the rest of the cast does. They should develop the habit of using the master list and not rely on memory from the beginning to the end. Once they are accustomed to their jobs, they will perform expertly just as your young actors will. One of our youngsters overcame a fear of heights and learned to install our three overhead microphones while standing on a ladder. After he came down from the ladder, he said, "I was so scared my knees were shaking, but I knew that was my job!" Be certain to emphasize to the rest of the children how important this job is to the success of the show. The stage crew children must have a feeling of their importance too!

Props

The term "props" is a nickname for "properties" and refers to items used on stage other than scenery, such as suitcases, baskets, musical instruments, books, etc. They add realism to the story, and they can be either borrowed or made. As you work on your script, try to eliminate any props you know will be impossible to find. Then make a complete list of those props you will need.

Present the list at your parents' meeting in October, and you will be pleased to find that your parents will already have many of the items at home. From that point, the search will fan out via the parents to friends and relatives who may be able to help. For one of our shows, we needed a light saddle. I knew a regular saddle was too heavy for the 10-year-old boy who was to carry it onstage. A parent was able to round up a pony saddle for us. We have borrowed rocking chairs, suitcases, a guitar, violin, cornet. Need a bed? Some family is certain to have a roll-away cot. Covered with a bedspread, it is ideal and it can be stored easily backstage when not in use. For *Oklahoma!* we wanted a real bale of hay. Luckily, one of our parents intended to reseed his suburban lawn that spring and planned to cover the grass seed with hay, so he bought the bale and loaned it to us before he used it. The laundry cart in our production of *Annie* was actually a mail cart borrowed from the local post office. How's that for community cooperation?

What you cannot borrow, you must make. In *Annie Get Your Gun,* Annie is adopted into a Sioux Indian tribe. During the ceremony Chief Sitting Bull places around Annie's neck a necklace so heavy that she staggers under its weight. Our necklace was made from a kit ordered from a Boy Scout catalog and had plastic bear claws and small pieces of rabbit fur attached to a leather thong. Although the necklace looked heavy and our Annie's knees buckled when it was put over her head, it was actually light as a feather. In *The King and I* one character was supposed to wear a monocle, a difficult item to find. We purchased a large wooden cafe curtain ring, painted it black and attached a black cord to it. From the audience's view, our monocle was quite realistic, even without glass in it.

The same show called for an oriental gong. We rigged a large brass tray to a stand and the actor hit the tray with the heel of his hand instead of a mallet to avoid denting the tray. It looked as impressive as the sabers in the sword dance, which were actually made from plywood. I drew a pattern on brown wrapping paper of scimitar-type sabers. Using the pattern a father cut four of them from scrap plywood which he had on hand. We painted them gold and the dancers looked dashing wielding such weapons on stage.

For *Oklahoma!* we decided to have six girls do a maypole dance. We attached an 8 ft. × 2 in. wooden pole to a base made of a wooden orange crate covered with cardboard, painted and weighted with a cinder block. We cut a hole in the crate and slipped the end of the pole down into it. We purchased grosgrain ribbon in two colors, red and white. Each ribbon was ten feet long and stapled to the top of the pole. Our maypole could be transported easily on and off the stage by our young stage crew members. The dance was a huge hit with the audience as the girls braided their ribbons around the pole!

How about two huge rocks, made of papier-mâché, yet sturdy enough to sit on? First we built a wooden base resembling a 12-inch cube or stool. The stool was covered with chicken wire, formed into a very irregularly shaped mound. As a class project the children covered the chicken wire with many layers of papier-mâché. When it was dry, a volunteer painted it to look like a rock, using grey paint with black accents! When a child sat on it, he was careful to sit in the center of the top, where the wooden stool was right under the surface. We constructed two of these, and used them in more than one show when the scene depicted the outdoors.

Papier-mâché rocks

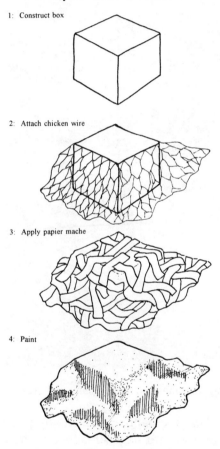

1: Construct box

2: Attach chicken wire

3: Apply papier mache

4: Paint

The raw materials for most of your props can be found in someone's basement. Collect throwaways such as pieces of Styrofoam, poster board, foam rubber, carpeting, large ice-cream containers, scrap lumber. The most versatile material, though, is good, old, reliable cardboard. It can be cut into any shape, painted with school tempera paint and is self-supporting and available in abundance at no cost to you. The boxes used to ship major appliances such as refrigerators are ideal. Cut the cardboard with your wallpapering tool, the razor blade cutter. Handle the cardboard in the same way as that used for the train seats, mentioned in the "Scenery" chapter. Using cardboard we have made everything from potted ferns to fences to tombstones.

For *Oklahoma!* our scenery designer created a butter churn from two five-gallon ice-cream containers donated by a local ice-cream store, an old broom and a little ingenuity. She glued the tops on the containers and then glued the two containers together, one on top of the other. The old broom handle was threaded through holes in the containers. What remained

The costume, scenery, props and acting combine to make the scene believable.

of the broom straw at the bottom kept the handle from slipping out and also from making noise as it hit the hard stage surface. She then covered the sides of the "churn" with poster board and painted on a wood grain pattern using two shades of brown paint and a black felt-tipped marker for accent. It looked so realistic that a nearby high school borrowed it the next year for its production of the same show.

A light cardboard, such as poster board, is ideal for props requir-

A butter churn made from ice-cream containers

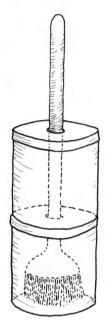 

ing molding or curling. We manufactured permanently frozen ice-cream cones from poster board and Styrofoam pears. We cut 12-inch circles from poster board, painted them light brown and then cut a single slit from one edge into the center. The circles were then curled and glued into a cone shape and the Styrofoam pears, painted pastel ice-cream colors, were glued into the paper cones. They looked good enough to eat!

Jean, our scenery designer, let her imagination run wild over the finale for our production of *Annie Get Your Gun*. We decided that the finale should resemble a circus parade. Obviously, live horses and elephants were out, but we wanted to give the audience a feeling of the rich pageantry of a parade. The solution seemed to be having the cast members carry something colorful and festive. But what?

While the director choreographed a marching finale routine for 16 children, Jean designed something we nicknamed "Flags and Fluffies." Each child would carry a four-foot stick (one-inch square) cut from old furring strips and painted turquoise. At the top of eight of the sticks would be our flags. No one ever guessed that the Flags had once been an umbrella covering. A donated umbrella was dismantled and the red and blue fabric sections taken apart, resulting in

The "Fluffies" made a showy accessory for the *Annie Get Your Gun* finale.

four red and four blue triangular rayon pieces 18 inches long and 12 inches at the wide end. Jean sewed them into pennants, slipping a triangular piece of poster board in for stiffness and tacked them to the four-foot stick. For interest she added a short thong with four feathers at the top.

At the top of the other eight sticks were the Fluffies, round cardboard discs with fluffy feathers radiating six inches out from the edges all the way around. Jean cut two 11-inch cardboard discs for each Fluffy and used a black felt-tipped marker to draw a thunderbird design on each. The children painted the discs with red and turquoise tempera paint. Jean then glued the turquoise feathers onto the back of one of the discs for each Fluffy. The fuzzy feathers were attached, overlapping along the edge, with plenty of white glue and allowed to dry overnight. The feathered and unfeathered discs were tacked back-to-back at the top of the stick. The Flags and Fluffies survived countless rehearsals and made a colorful addition to the big finale. The children sang "There's No Business Like Show Business" and marched, carrying these bright props overhead. Their audience responded with wild applause and cheers!

Sound Effects

Fortunately, most Broadway musicals appropriate for children do not require many sound effects. The few that are called for can be handled with ease. A thunderstorm, for example, can be simulated by a stage crew member rattling a thin piece of sheet aluminum off-stage. Church bells can be created by using metal pipe cut in different lengths. String the pipes on a piece of cord, knotting the cord to separate them, and have the stage crew "play" the pipes using a drum-stick or mallet.

The stickiest problem we ever dealt with was the gunshot sound effect for *Annie Get Your Gun*. Had it been an adult production, we would have simply used a starter gun with blank cartridges, but the thought of a ten-year-old with anything resembling a real gun in her hand sent shivers up our spines, so we looked for a safe and cheap alternative. You will find that many adult theater techniques are not acceptable for use with children.

For the clay pigeon shooting scene, the actors wore toy guns and holsters. Someone offstage would clap two wooden blocks together at the moment the gun was "fired." The actor would yell, "Pull!" for the clay pigeon to be released and fire his gun toward stage right by simulating a recoil at the same moment the blocks were clapped together. It soon became apparent that the children would not be able to synchronize the clap with the recoil. The children tried using caps in their guns, but caps were too unreliable. As mentioned in the directing chapter, the problem was ultimately solved by changing the audience's view of the actors firing the guns. By having the guns fired toward them instead of stage right, the audience could not detect those times when the clap did not exactly match the recoil. The shot was never as loud as we would have liked. Later a professional sound effects man told me that a believable gunshot can be made by using a snare drum. Lay one drumstick from the center of the drumhead to the outer rim. Hold the drumstick tight and strike it sharply with the other drumstick. It is much louder than clapping two blocks of wood together and just as safe. However, your problem with timing the shot to the recoil would still be the same.

If you need the sound of a train or something else that is hard to simulate, you may be able to make a tape recording yourself and play it near a microphone backstage at the appropriate moment. Of course, professional sound effects tapes are available, and most companies that sell them will send you a free catalog on request. Keep in mind that tape recorders take up valuable space backstage and require an adult to time the sound just right. We have never had to resort to the use of tapes.

Lights

If you have a curtained stage, you will probably have onstage lights and footlights already installed. They will be operated from a control panel backstage by your stage manager. Some schools own a large spotlight that must be operated from the audience area by your young lights technician. You are fortunate indeed if you have such facilities, for your lighting problems will be nonexistent.

If you don't have these features, you will have to come up with some stage lights, not only to enable your audience to see the show but also to create darkened breaks between acts for scenery changes if your stage has no curtain. To create natural lighting for your actors, the light must come from a source situated as high as possible. Sunlight does, after all, come from above, placing the shadows of the face in the expected places. Stage lights placed at eye level will cause your actors to squint. Lights from below, when used by themselves, create a ghoulish look, and unless you are doing a Halloween play, that is probably not the look for which you are striving. Therefore, if you can find any way to mount lights on or near the ceiling, do it. Your parents may have some good ideas for this.

If that is not possible and if you need portable lights for your "road show," consider our first system, which served admirably until we were able to upgrade. For your first no-budget show, try to borrow from parents five spotlights with fixtures and mount them on a heavy 6 × 36-inch board. The middle three spotlights will point straight ahead to light the center of the stage. The two on the outside will angle toward the front corners of the stage. Someone you know may have an old floodlight bar from the days of movie cameras and be willing to donate it. Unfortunately, floodlights have a short life span, so replace them with longer lasting spotlights as they burn out. Wire the cords to an on-off switch and an electrical plug available at hardware stores.

The entire lights assembly board must be placed as high as possible, so search your school for a tall audiovisual cart, usually four feet high, on which to place the board. A better plan is to build an open rectangular box to place on top of the cart. This arrangement

Lights board attached to support box on audiovisual cart

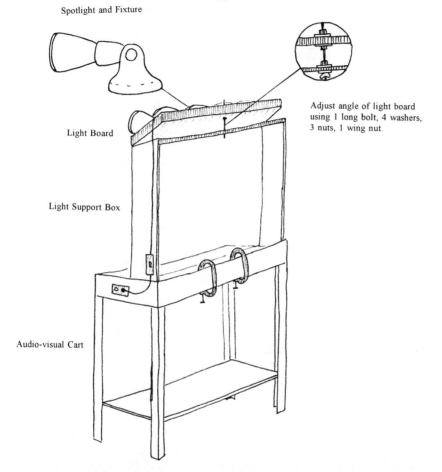

Spotlight and Fixture

Adjust angle of light board using 1 long bolt, 4 washers, 3 nuts, 1 wing nut.

Light Board

Light Support Box

Audio-visual Cart

will raise the light board even higher. Ours was three feet wide, four feet high and one foot deep. Borrowed C-clamps secured the box to the cart. As shown in the illustration, a long bolt with a special arrangement of washers and nuts enabled us to adjust the light board to the right angle for whatever stage we were using. The wire to the control switch was elongated so that the lights technician could reach it. The light board was plugged into the plug on the cart and the cart cord was plugged into the wall outlet. We taped the long cord to the floor so that excited youngsters in our audience would not trip over it.

The lights were situated near the center of the first row of the audience. The lights technician sat beside it, the only person authorized to touch the switch. He had to keep his script beside him at all

Footlights shielded by black aluminum

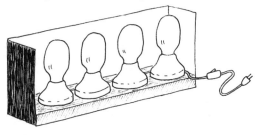

times to ensure that he turned the lights on and off at the right moments. Our young lights technician underlined his cue lines in red.

When we graduated to the new stage/music room at our school, we were able to use the room ceiling lights as our overheads. One switch would turn on lights to illuminate only the front of the stage. When a second switch was turned on, the entire stage was lit. A volunteer built two portable footlights, an addition that improved our lighting capabilities immensely. Each footlight has four ceramic light fixtures screwed to a board. Each has a sheet of aluminum attached to screen the audience from the lights, silver on the inside and painted black on the outside. One footlight has a plug so the two can be linked together. Both have an in-line switch and plug. With these two light sources, we can manage almost any light requirement. In *The Wizard of Oz*, when Dorothy, Scarecrow, Tin Woodman, and Lion came to call on the Wizard, we used a darkened stage and a borrowed strobe light. The effect was just what we were looking for!

To indicate nighttime and yet allow the audience to see what the action was, as in the opening scene of *Annie* when the orphans are asleep, we turned on only the lights at the front of the stage and left the rest of the area in darkness. It worked beautifully.

When we were producing *The Wizard of Oz*, we pondered long and hard how to suggest the idea of a tornado. We finally decided to blink all stage lights in rapid succession, over and over, as everyone on stage rushed around, calling that a twister was coming. Such a simple solution, but it was one of the most effective things we ever devised in the use of lights.

12

Programs and Photographs

It is a month before the show, and rehearsals on the stage are moving along well. It is time to think of the other things that will go into making your play a success. Every detail must be just right, and the children should be involved in those details.

Programs

You must plan the program for your play. Naturally, the body of the program will include a listing of the acts and scenes, the songs to be sung in each and the names of all the children who have worked on the play.

What will the program cover look like? It is fun to ask the children to enter a program cover design contest. I describe the contest to the children, explaining what makes a good cover. We want a simple design in which the name of the play is included. For printing purposes, the sketch must be done in fine line black pen in exactly the size of our program, 5½ × 8½ inches. The children may discuss the contest with their families and get ideas from them, but the actual artwork must be their own. They may submit more than one entry. I give them several days to work on their designs at home. Then they are collected and turned over to our judge, usually our scenery designer. She chooses a winner, and that design becomes our cover. Sometimes part of a runner-up design can be used elsewhere in the program. We usually have a drawing on the back of the program to honor another child-artist.

The program must also include the names of everyone else who

171

A program design contest among students
resulted in this handsome cover

made the play possible. Carefully keep a list of every person who has helped in any way over the months. All who have contributed effort outside of making their own child's costume must be mentioned in the program. Check and double-check that list to make sure no one is forgotten. List the names according to the kind of help given, such as makeup, props, etc. If parents have helped in more than one area, list their names under each category. If someone has signed up to assist in a job not yet needed, such as transportation of children or scenery, be sure that person's name is included. Your play would not be happening without the assistance of those wonderful, busy people, and you want to recognize each one of them. We always add a one-page insert to our program, listing each person who has helped, and everyone is always pleased to be remembered in this way. I even list the names of noncast children who loan us costumes or props. Our program insert for *The Music Man* is shown here.

Because you have the most complete knowledge of the play, the cast and adult volunteers, you will type or at least proofread the program before it is printed. Omitting a name is even worse than misspelling a name. Be sure your final copy is exactly right.

How will you print your program? The least-expensive way may be by using the copier at school with ordinary 20 lb. bond paper or heavier stock. Another possibility is a printing program in your high school's vocational education department. There it may be possible to have the program printed for the cost of paper alone. We were able to do this once. The high school students had a real printing job to do, and we had a good-looking program on heavier paper stock. Another resource may be a local printer who may be willing to do the job at minimal cost. Be sure to give him credit on the program. "Programs printed through the courtesy of Vienna Print Shop."

We usually have five hundred programs printed for each play. We hand these out to our audience only on the nights of the community performances. It is too expensive to use them at the other school performances. The distribution of the programs is another chance to make four more children with minor parts feel important. These youngsters, in costume and make up, distribute programs to our audience as they arrive on the big night. They are always overjoyed to be chosen for this task!

Program insert for *The Music Man*

BACKSTAGE ASSISTANCE

Assistant Director
Barbara Butler

Musical Director
Kathy Quarles

Director
Beverly Ross

We would like to thank all our fifth grade parents for their help and cooperation in the production of this show. We could not have a successful play without them.

The following people deserve special thanks for their extra time and effort. Some do not even have a fifth grade child.

Set Design: JEAN DURGIN

Costume Coordinator: JOANN DONNELLY

Stage Manager: BARBARA BUTLER
        Assistants: Bert Eckhoff, Mrs. Fortune, Mr. Minor

Choreographer: BEVERLY ROSS

Cast Photographer: DICK DURGIN

Programs: JUSTIN DONNELLY

Dance Instructors: Mrs. Eckhoff, Mrs. Roth, Mrs. Lee.

Costumes: JOANN DONNELLY, Mrs. Ross, Mrs. Whitehead, Mrs. Skidmore, Mrs. McCade, Mrs. Woods, Mrs. Thomas, Mrs. Jonas, Mrs. Clark.

Makeup: JANICE MARTIN, Mrs. Steele, Mrs. O'Malley, Mrs. Nolte, Mrs. Miller, Mrs. Hannan, Mrs. Gannet, Mrs. O'Brady, Mrs. Hardin, Mrs. Marr, Mrs. Lyons, Mrs. James, Mrs. Bruce, Mrs. Joseph.

Carpentry: DICK DURGIN, Mr. Warren, Mr. Harvey, Mr. March.

Scenery Help: JEAN DURGIN, Mrs. Maroney, Mrs. Taub, Mr. Sumter, Mrs. Hackett.

Program insert for *The Music Man*

Props: GERI SIMMONS, Mrs. Talbot, Mrs. Swanson, Mr. Wong, Mr. Zungan.

Publicity: JOYCE YEAGER, Mrs. Woodward, Mrs. Pointer.

Backstage Supervision: LAUREN WISOR, Mrs. Dalby, Mr. Benson, Mr. Cramer, Mrs. Kellog, Mrs. Curtin, Mr. Alexander.

Cast Party & Gifts: LAURIE CUTTER, Mrs. Dalton, Mrs. Swanson, Mrs. Taub, Mrs. Battle, Mrs. Dalby, Mrs. Wong, Mrs. Cramer.

Diction Coach: BERT ECKHOFF

Printing: Mr. Cummins, Mrs. Neal, Mr. Dabny, Mrs. Vaughn.

Auditions: Mrs. Ross, Mrs. Butler, Mrs. Quarles, Mrs. Durgin, Mrs. Donnelly.

Financial Support: Cedar Park PTA

Special thanks to the office staff of Cedar Park School, and especially to Mary Pace, Principal, for all their help and support during the last three months.

Programs have been printed through the courtesy of Justin Donnelly and Donnelly's Printing & Graphics.

Photographs of the Show

A cast photographer is essential when putting on a play with children. So many priceless moments must be caught on film. Find a willing volunteer who has a good 35 mm camera and preferably a zoom lens. Because the children wear costumes and makeup during dress rehearsal, that is the perfect time for your photographer to walk around snapping pictures unencumbered by an audience. He must be sure to include all children in the pictures no matter how small their parts. He should also snap a couple of photos of the lights technician if you are using one and stage crew if they are not also in the cast. He will take more pictures of leading and secondary leading characters than the other children. These children participate in more of the action of the story and, therefore, tend to be photographed more often.

Before beginning our dress rehearsal we pose the entire cast and crew at the front of the stage for a group picture. Children whose only involvement is painting scenery are included in this group. Our cast photographer takes several photos, and the best one is usually printed up by the adults of the Cast Party Committee, and a copy is given to each child at the cast party. The print is usually mounted on a colorful piece of bristol board. It makes a wonderful souvenir.

Your photographer may choose to take pictures during an evening

Curly is annoyed by Laurie's brush-off in *Oklahoma!*

performance for the community as well. He should be assigned a reserved seat, front and center. There are usually ceremonies at the final performance of our shows that do not occur during any other performance. Our children always secretly collect money for gifts for the director, assistant director, musical director and other adults who have worked so hard to make their show a success. When these gifts are presented, your photographer should have some film left in his camera to record the excitement.

Once, during the curtain calls, our leading man leaned over and kissed his leading lady on the cheek. There were over six hundred people in the audience, many with their own cameras, and not a single one got a picture of that unexpected kiss!

I always pay for the film and developing of all pictures taken by the cast photographer. He is doing all of us a great favor by giving his time and talent to an important job. He should not be required to bear the financial burden of the task as well. Because I have paid for the pictures, they are mine to keep when the show is over. I gladly assume this monetary responsibility.

After having all the film developed, I post the best pictures in the hall outside my classroom and at the cast party so that students and their families may order copies. The task of taking the orders, having copies made and distributing them is a big one. If you can recruit a photo chairperson, it will be a huge help to you. Meanwhile, I check local photo dealers to find the best price for reprints of our pictures. I then send home a letter inviting parents to view all of the snapshots and order those they and their children would like to keep as souvenirs. I have developed an order form for these photos that I use each year. I designate each roll with a letter—Roll A, Roll B, and so on. The pictures are numbered A-1, A-2, etc. to correspond to the numbers on the negatives. The order form looks like this.

Picture Order Form.   **Name:**_____

A-1____	B-1____	C-1____	D-1____	Column 1____
A-2____	B-2____	C-2____	D-2____	Column 2____
A-3____	B-3____	C-3____	D-3____	Column 3____
A-4____	B-4____	C-4____	D-4____	Column 4____
A-5____	B-5____	C-5____	D-5____	Total_____
A-6____	B-6____	C-6____	D-6____	x_____
A-7____	B-7____	C-7____	D-7____	(cost per print)
A-8____	B-8____	C-8____	D-8____	Total
A-9____	B-9____	C-9____	D-9____	Cost $_____
Total____	Total____	Total____	Total____	

Either you or your photo chairperson collects the money at the time the child orders pictures. Then the huge bookkeeping job begins. Use a blank order form and tally all the orders, checking and double-checking to avoid errors. One year I found that our fifth-grade families had ordered a total of over one thousand prints of our snapshots. This shows how important they consider these pictures of our plays to be.

Combining individual orders into a master order and submitting it to a local photo shop is only half the job. When the order comes back, it must be distributed correctly. I use inexpensive white letter envelopes. I write a child's name on the front of each envelope and the numbers of every snapshot she ordered, copying this information from the original order form. As I take the snapshots out of the developer's envelopes, I write the number on the back of each. I then put them in the appropriate white envelopes, checking off numbers as the pictures are inserted. It is therefore quite easy to see at a glance where any mistakes have occurred, and reorders can be made if necessary. The envelopes are handed out to the children in school the next day.

Videotapes

Over the years parents began taping the shows with their home video cameras. Although still photos are wonderful, nothing compares to actually being able to see the action and hear the singing. Our school system has a vocational education program in Television Communications. The high schoolers in that program learn how to operate field and studio cameras, microphones, videotape recorders and all the other equipment used by television stations. We learned that senior students in the program could come to our school and tape the evening performance for a modest fee. They could then make copies of the tapes for our children for the cost of the tape. We decided to give it a try and it turned out to be a fine arrangement. Our families were able to relive the show through the videotape and the TV students received real on-the-job experience.

The pictures that I keep of each of our plays are among my most treasured possessions. Every single snapshot has its own story to tell. What precious, wonderful children are pictured there. I will never forget a single one. I will always have my show albums to enjoy and to help me remember!

13

The Performance

The excitement is building—in you, in the parents, but most of all, in the children. They have spent at least three months in rehearsal. You and the parents have spent that time on all of the other details to make the show a success. Your first performance will be for the rest of the students in your school. You have cleared the date with the school principal who by this time is almost as enthusiastic as you are.

Have the children bring all of their costumes to school several days before the first show. They will be hanging from the chalkboard, from the window frames, everywhere—unless you are able to borrow two large, portable clothes racks, one for boys' costumes and one for girls'. Double-check each costume as it is brought to school. If you have a number of identical costumes, such as our Indian costumes, put a large name tag on each of those hangers. All hats, shoes and other accessories should be in plastic shopping bags with handles and the handles looped over the tops of the hangers so that each child's costume is all together. In working with youngsters this age, you will find that many are careless about keeping track of their belongings.

Remind them that it is their responsibility to keep their things together. You have enough to do without having to hunt for a stray shoe just before a performance!

Our first performance is usually scheduled for 9:00 A.M. I arrive at school at 7:30 and set up the makeup table in the hall. The children arrive at 8:00, as does the parent Makeup Committee. We set aside my classroom as a dressing room for boys and a separate classroom for the girls. There is an adult in each, to maintain order among excited children. The boys seem much more excited than the girls and therefore tend toward mischief, so I station myself in that room. The boys quickly recover from the modesty that my presence creates, especially if they find that I'm there but not watching them change

179

clothes. Our assistant director is in the girls' dressing room. Each of us is armed with safety pins, needle and thread, a hairbrush and facial tissue.

The stage crew is usually the first to be dressed, so they immediately report to the makeup table and then go to the stage area to set up the scenery and props for the opening scene. As soon as the soloists are dressed they report to makeup, going to the front of the line if one has formed. Then they report to the musical director for a warm-up session.

Preshow Jitters

As soon as all the boys are dressed, my classroom is opened so that all children who have completed makeup, girls as well as boys, can assemble there. All children except the stage crew report to my classroom no later than 15 minutes before show time. Be prepared for signs of nervousness, especially in your main characters. It is common for a child to have an attack of diarrhea or nausea during all the preparation excitement. This occurs most often before the first (student) performance and to a lesser extent before the first evening performance for the community. After that, the children are experienced performers, and nerves are not a problem. All you can do is make sure they have access to the bathroom and assure them that their feelings are entirely normal. It seems to help them to know that professional actors suffer in the same way.

I remember one shy child who had a dance solo to perform. During the first evening performance, as the time approached for her to capture the spotlight, she became more and more nervous. Her hands actually shook! With her parents and all those other people from the community watching, she knew that she had to go on—there was simply no way to avoid it. As she started to dance, her nerves lessened somewhat. She did a beautiful job, without a single mistake. After the dance was over and she had exited the stage, her face told her feelings. She knew that she had conquered a huge obstacle—her own fear—and she had done what she was supposed to do. She felt she was ten feet tall! Her pride, her elation and her self-confidence were priceless to her. I am sure that child will remember her experience even after she has grown to adulthood.

The most extreme case of nerves that I ever observed was in a youngster who turned out to be one of the most talented children I

Our 60-pound dynamo in *The Music Man.*

have ever worked with. His nerves did not occur on the day of our performance for the students in our school. This particular year the news of our unusually fine show, *The Music Man,* spread even before our first performance. We were invited to put on a 20-minute segment for a group of 60 school principals from our county. This show was to be two weeks before our first scheduled performance. We thought we were ready, but we had not had as much time to rehearse as we had planned. The morning arrived, and this child's mother called me to say that he had been sick all night long but was determined to do his part. He arrived at school looking ghost-white! He spent much time in the bathroom, and he was a very sick young man. He kept assuring me that he could perform though. As I led the cast into the cafeteria where the show was to be held, Justin looked at me and said, "Don't worry, Mrs. Ross. I'm all right now." He was! What a sensation he created! Those principals, from high schools, junior highs and elementary schools, sat there openmouthed. They could not believe that elementary school children could put on a production like that, and Justin amazed them the most. He belted out "Trouble" and "Seventy-six Trombones" with every ounce of energy he had in his 60-pound body! It was unbelievable! Those principals still talk about it. Justin, who has performed many times in many different shows since then, has conquered his nerves for all times. In later years, he joined a rock group that traveled up and down the east coast of the United States, performing for colleges and universities. Today he has his own recording studio. He's come a long way since fifth grade!

This brings up another point. I am frequently asked, "Have you ever had a child too sick to perform?" My answer is NO! I remember our king in *The King and I*, who was running a 101-degree temperature the evening of our community performance, yet he did a magnificent job. Then there was Marian, in *The Music Man*, who went on stage, performed a scene, left the stage, found a bathroom where she vomited and then went back on stage in time for her next cue. I have had children absent from school because of illness, whose parents brought them for a performance and then took them back home and put them to bed. I remember a parent who postponed her child's tonsillectomy until after the show was over! One child's family, due to move permanently to another state, postponed the move until he'd participated in every single performance. There have been several cases of parents postponing having their child's braces put on until after the show for fear the appliance would interfere with the child's diction. Somehow the theater motto "The show must go on" seems to carry over to children and their parents as well as professionals.

The Pep Talk

Getting back to the first performance, have all of the children assemble in your classroom before going to the stage. You must give them last-minute instructions and a pep talk. I always remind my cast members to pause for audience laughter or applause before reciting the next line. I stress superior behavior when not on stage. There is nothing more distracting to an audience than noise backstage. Then I tell them about their audience that day. A student audience of younger children will think these actors extremely good as they try to imagine themselves on a stage, performing for a large group. Sixth graders, in the audience, who did a big show the year before, know the work involved. They will appreciate the efforts of these children, though they may secretly be hoping that this show is not as good as their show. This is perfectly normal. I urge the children to do their very best, to show the sixth graders that they are capable too.

For the first evening performance my pep talk is slightly different. In describing that audience, I tell the children that these people are mostly their parents and friends. If a mistake is made on stage, they will excuse it, understanding that the actors are children. I tell the cast that we want to make the audience amazed at the quality of our show and our actors. I always challenge every cast before every performance—"Let's show them we are THE BEST!" And they do!

For the second evening performance, the children's nerves have all but disappeared. I tell them, "Okay, kids, this one's for *you*! Go out there and have a *ball*! Do your very best, because you want to remember a perfect performance for the rest of your lives."

Adjusting to a Larger Stage

The student performance over, the children and adults turn their attention to those biggest of all shows—the evening ones for our community. This will be true show-off time! Years ago, before the music room/stage was built at our school, we chose to use the stage at the local junior high school. That meant we had to learn to use a different stage and its technical facilities. The parents on the scenery and transportation committees had to pack up and haul the scenery, props and other paraphernalia to our new location and set it up for our use. Costumes had been sent home with the children after the student performance. This time they were to dress at home and arrive at the

Ali Hakim having a ball in *Oklahoma!*

junior high school to have their makeup applied. We followed this practice when we used our new music room/stage also.

Our first day of practice on that new stage could be described in one word: chaos! It would have been easy to become discouraged. The children had so much new information to absorb, and they were so excited that they seemed to pay very little attention to anything I said. The thing that was most difficult for them to learn was how to utilize a stage that was more than twice the size of the one on which they had been practicing. Group scenes were especially difficult. The children huddled in small, close groups instead of spreading out to take advantage of the large area. I sometimes put masking tape on the stage floor to help them remember where to stand.

They also had to make an adjustment in timing. If a child had been accustomed to entering on a particular cue word in order to reach his designated place before he spoke, he found that due to the wider stage his cue word must be changed. I felt it was essential that, on that first chaotic day, the entire play be rehearsed from start to finish. I had to stand far back in the audience area to be sure that the children could be heard and understood.

We needed to make major corrections in dance numbers because of the larger stage. We had only three days of rehearsal on this stage, and the children had spent months practicing in a much smaller area. The masking tape markings on the stage floor gave them something on which to depend, and they quickly adapted their spacing to the larger area.

Was it worth all the trouble of hauling equipment, a chaotic rehearsal day, and learning to use a larger stage just to accommodate a large audience comfortably? The answer is an unqualified yes! If half the audience had to stand, they would not enjoy our show nearly as much. I would not go to even a professional performance if I knew I would have to stand for the entire show. Yet, as our reputation grew, and our audience grew along with it, they filled every seat, and the rest stood for our entire performance. Apparently they decided that standing was better than missing the show! What a compliment to our wonderful children!

When our own music room/stage was constructed, however, I must admit that all of the adults involved heaved a huge sigh of relief! The children had practiced on our stage for the last month of rehearsals, and they knew exactly what to do. No relearning was necessary.

We didn't even have to take our show "on the road" because other schools sent their children to attend our student performance. Perhaps we weren't serving as many children as we would have if we'd performed for their entire student body, but those particularly interested could have attended either of our community performances. We had already added a second evening performance to accommodate the crowds.

Reserved Seats

The parents of our cast members have put so much time and effort into this play that we guarantee them a seat as close to the stage as possible. My seat is on the front row next to the one reserved for the cast photographer. The parents and relatives of our male and female leads are also seated in the front row. For seating of the other children's families, we have worked out a reserved seat system. Prior to show night I take a count from each cast member of how many adults will be attending from his or her family. I do not include children in the family because they always seem to prefer to sit on the floor in front of the first row of chairs. I then make a large name tag bearing the child's last name for each adult who is expected. One hour before curtain time, the children arrive at school, dressed in the costumes they will wear first in the play. All other costumes are already hung backstage. The children pick up their name tags, choose seats for their families, and place one tag on each chair. They then report to the makeup room where the parent makeup crew waits to do its job. As the audience arrives, parents and family members look for their name tags and sit in those seats. Other members of the audience must take seats not previously reserved. We charge no admission to our productions, so tickets are unnecessary, but we happily accept donations to help us cover expenses.

Children who are backstage awaiting their turns to go on should have assigned places to sit—on the floor because every available chair is needed for the audience. The only exception might be for a leading lady who couldn't sit on the floor for fear that her costume would be wrinkled. Such was the case with the magnificent creations worn by our Mrs. Anna in *The King and I*.

You need at least two volunteer parents backstage whose only assignment is to help control the children. Our stage manager will help children change costumes. If she needs additional aid, one of the backstage parents is there to help while the other remains visible to the children, watching behavior and gently correcting where necessary.

Crazy Cue Cards

I am never backstage during any performance. I am always seated in the center front row of the audience, where the children can see me and my cue cards easily. During the months of rehearsals when a child made a mistake or needed stage direction from me, I was able to give it verbally. In performances this is impossible. Yet these are children, and they still need my support and encouragement during the play. My cue cards work beautifully and the audience never knows of their existence. In my lap I have a group of white tagboard cards measuring at least seven by ten inches. I write my messages on these cards with heavy black felt-tipped markers so that the children on stage are able to read them. On each card is printed only one or two words of direction, but the children know what they mean.

Many of my cards read: *Loud, Slow, Face Front, Move Center, Sing!, Look Excited, Smile!* If a child is standing too far back on stage, I hold up the "Move Front" card, right in front of my chest where my back shields it from others behind me. The child sees the sign and gradually moves toward the front of the stage. Perhaps the stage is full of children and someone enters with exciting news or sings an exciting song. If the children do not react as they should, I hold up my "Look Excited" sign, and they respond accordingly. I insist that my actors and actresses smile at all times on stage, except when something sad happens in the action of the story. After a while, they forget to smile, so out comes the "Smile" card. This card is used more than any other, so pretty soon it produces no results in some children. Then I bring out the drawing of a smile face, and that helps for a while. Then some forget again. So, my next card is a surprise to them, one that they have not seen before. It has a horrible frowning face drawn on it. I try to save this one for the finale, because they not only smile when they see it, but some almost laugh! That certainly adds oomph to the finale! It is always wise to keep a few blank cards and your marker handy for the unexpected situation that develops and needs attention. Once I had to write, "Tell Mrs. Butler that mikes are not working!" Then there was the time when my sign read, "Brad, zip your fly!"

"Break a Leg"

Three minutes before curtain time our musical director sits at the piano and begins to play the overture. Our audience quiets down in anticipation of the beginning of the show. We, who have worked so hard on so many phases of this play, know that we have done all we can to help the children, and now it is all up to them. The curtain opens, and the first line is spoken by a very nervous youngster. After the first few minutes of the first scene, you can see the children visibly relax. They are having a wonderful time!

A very interesting phenomenon appears at the first evening performance each year. Because many of the humorous lines in a Broadway show are not understood by most young children, the laughter at the performance for the school children has been minimal. Adults, however, understand the lines so much better and respond with laughter in the proper places. As the children on stage notice the laughter where it has not been before, they begin to react to it. They come alive more than ever before. They exaggerate gestures or expressions—they become such "hams" that they are priceless! One girl in *The Music Man* had a line about a bunion on her foot. She wore a long skirt, and until that evening performance she had simply moved her foot around under her skirt as she said her line. For that adult audience she outdid herself. She'd received a few laughs earlier in the scene and apparently decided she liked it! As she described her bunion she hoisted her skirt halfway to her knee and moved that foot all over the place. It was hilarious, and her audience roared! On that evening I always see an entirely different show than ever before, even though I've sat through three months of rehearsals. It happens every year!

As the show progresses, the audience hangs on every word. They laugh in the right places. They applaud every song. They soon forget that the actors are children. They become carried away by the story, and only after the finale is over do they realize where they are and who is performing. That thunderous applause is something those children will never forget. As they go into their encore, their audience continues to clap, finally rising to its feet in a standing ovation to these wonderful children! There are no words to describe the feelings in the hearts of each member of the audience. Can you imagine what those children on stage are feeling! One boy said, "I felt like I was standing on a real Broadway stage." Another said with absolute wonder, "They love us!" Whenever someone asks me why I put on children's plays, I can only think of that moment when the curtain closes.

When the finale ends, your children will have a feeling of accomplishment that they never experienced before. This is no exaggeration. No well-done school assignment, no winning baseball game, no flawless piano recital can come close to equaling the elation of working so long and hard on a project and then having so many people recognize your efforts with their applause and praise.

Three months before, the idea of singing and acting in front of a room full of people was a scary thing. These children wondered if they would ever be able to do it. Now the performances are behind them, and they know how good they are! The feeling of self-confidence gained by every child in the cast is something no one can ever take away from them. It lives with them forever, and it influences everything they undertake in later life. You have helped them to achieve it. You know what it is worth to them.

Suddenly, when they are taking their bows, it occurs to the children that their show is over. They will never perform it again. For some, especially the leads and secondary leads, this is a devastating thought. Many a "leading lady," and even a few "leading men," have come out on stage to take a bow with tears in their eyes. It happens so often, and yet there doesn't seem to be anything I can do about it.

I remember the time when the children didn't wait for the "leads" to begin the tears. The very first child on stage for a bow had glistening eyes. From then on things just got worse! When it came time for the children to give the hardworking adult volunteers the gifts the parents had selected and purchased for us, each had a little speech prepared to accompany the presentation. One child came to the microphone, package in hand, and sobbing as though her heart would break. "I can't do it," she managed to utter, and handed the package to another child standing nearby. In later years, we would always think of that group as "the crying cast."

When it is my turn to receive my gift, and then to say a few words to the audience, I always make sure that they understand the tears are because the children don't want their show to be over. I certainly don't want them to think we've been beating anyone backstage! The audience understands. In fact, there are more than a few moist eyes in the audience when they realize what this experience has meant to their children.

Speaking of presentations, there is a story I feel compelled to relate. The parents planned it without my knowledge, so it was a surprise to me as well as to the children, and it unintentionally turned out to be one of the funniest things I ever saw!

The parents wanted to present each child with a flower to carry onstage when they were introduced after the show. Because of the time of year, daffodils were the chosen flower. I don't know what kind of trauma those poor flowers suffered beforehand, but as each was presented to a child, *many* had lost their blossoms, and the children received only the *stems*. Imagine the expression on a bewildered child's face when he or she is unexpectedly handed a flower *stem* to hold while walking to stage front, taking a bow, and stepping aside for another child to follow, stem in hand! Standing there, each looked around at the other children, most of whom were staring in bewilderment at their stems. A very few lucky ones stared at the flowers attached to their stems. You could almost see the wheels turning inside the child's head, and almost hear the tiny voice inside whispering, "*Someone* has lost their *mind*!" I laugh about it to this day!

After the final curtain, there is pandemonium backstage! Children cry, adults breathe an enormous sigh of relief, and parents begin to come through the curtain with words of congratulations, loving caresses and bouquets for their children. Belongings are quickly gathered up and loaded into cars. Then all cast members and their families adjourn to our school cafeteria for a stupendous cast party with gallons of punch and hundreds of cookies. Children collect each other's autographs on souvenir programs, and parents snap dozens of pictures. What an evening!

Cast Party

The cast party is handled exclusively by a parent committee. I am too busy with show details to think about it, and we always have a creative and willing chairperson and plenty of volunteers to help. It's fun to plan a party, a job that's familiar to them. About three weeks before the community performance, the party chairperson writes a letter to all cast members about the party and tells them that it will be held in our school cafeteria immediately following the evening performance. All cast members, their families and out-of-town relatives or friends are invited. (Once we had a father come all the way from Guam to see his son perform!) Each child is asked for a contribution to cover the cost of punch, napkins, cups and decorations, in addition to the gifts that will be given to each volunteer who does *not* have a child in the show. (Parents of children in the show are *expected* to help, so no gifts go to them.) There were usually eight volunteers, including the director, who received gifts, so a total sum of $10 was requested from each child's family to cover gifts and party expenses. In addition, each child is asked to contribute cookies or vegetables and dip to the party and to bring them to school on the day of the cast party. The committee's job is to decorate our cafeteria for the party, to arrange the punch and cookies on refreshment tables and to clean up after the party ends.

We order cocktail-size napkins, imprinted with the show name and date. The children love to have them as souvenirs of their show. One year our party was made even more authentic by the brainstorm of a few parents who created our own version of a *Variety*-type newspaper. Real Broadway show casts usually retire to the nearest pub to await nervously the arrival of the newspaper reviews of their shows. Of course, our reviews were written and printed far in advance of the party, but the children were thrilled to read seemingly hot-off-the-press accounts of their flawless performance that evening. The review even reported the standing ovation the children had received only an hour before. The author must have had a crystal ball. Our paper included a gossip column with humorous anecdotes that had occurred during the weeks of rehearsal. Each child received a copy as a surprise and a priceless souvenir.

Each child also receives a snapshot of the entire cast, taken by the cast photographer that first day of dress rehearsal, hurriedly printed in quantity and mounted on tagboard cut to size. These are also treasured souvenirs.

The children spend the entire time at the cast party stuffing food into their mouths (they'd been too nervous to eat dinner before the show) and gathering autographs on their programs from all the other cast members and the main adult volunteers.

Some Good
Things Never End

After the party, the young actors go home and reluctantly climb into bed. They are tired but proud and happy, and sleep comes slowly. I have received many notes from parents over the years. One says in part,

> As a teacher it was delightful to watch students begin to lose themselves in the character they were portraying. One could not help but notice students developing more confidence, greater self-esteem and a facility to work together on a new and creative venture. It was also obvious how much fun they had in the whole process!
>
> On behalf of all fifth grade students and parents, I want to thank you for your boundless energy, determination and persistence in creating such an outstanding production. You have given these fifth grade students a unique and magical experience, as well as memories for a lifetime.

Others told me of their child's reaction to the show. One in particular, which I will always keep, came from a parent of a very shy boy who played a minor character in our show. It says, in part:

> I would like to thank you for all that you have done for our children—all the planning, time, energy and work you have put into making our children such a success. I have seen the change in Willie day by day. The confidence, self-assurance and maturing that has come from being a part of *The Music Man*. They all have gained so much and you have been the one who has directed our children in achieving this. Friday night after we got home, Willie, tired but experiencing the satisfied feeling of success remarked, "Boy, Mom, I will remember tonight all my life!" I want to say Thank You so much.

This note always brings tears to my eyes. What greater reward is there in life than to give such happiness to a child?

What do the children say? Here are some examples.

Children's reactions to their show

"THE MUSIC MAN" & MY THOUGHTS

At auditions I was very nervous about singing. The next day I wondered if I would get a good part. On Monday I found out that I got a great part. I was so excited that I couldn't wait to tell my parents.

When winter vacation was over and we all went back to school I was looking forward to going to rehearsals. The first rehearsal was fun, so were the others. But when February was almost over and March was coming I got tired of it, day after day of after-school practicing. I thought that we were ready.

Finally the first dress rehearsal came, then the second, you have to admit that it was full of fun. The school performance was better. Thursday and Friday's night performances were the best. I loved the fun and the crowd's response. We were better than great. When the final performance was over and we gave out the gifts I thought back to the auditions, the rehearsals and all the hard work it took to do this. I said to myself, "I will never forget the greatest day of my life, today." I longed for us to do it again. At the cast party I felt sad but happy, we worked hard for a long time and it paid off.

This show has changed my life. I feel that I can accomplish anything now. I feel like I was 76 and now I'm 10. I feel great. I'm a totally new person. In my heart I will keep the memories of "The Music Man," a show that is unforgettable.

"The King and I"

I felt really nervous when we did our first performance at Thoreau I felt a little relaxed after the March of the Siamese Children. I really felt embarrassed but I soon got over that feeling. I wish we could go all around the world to do The King and I.

Oklahoma!

It was Tuesday January 2, I couldn't wait for school to end because we were having rehearsals that day. As rehearsals wore on we slowly got better and better. Finally we were going to dress rehearsals. It was *very* fun. Then it was our first performance. When I looked through the curtain I got nervous but as soon as I got on stage I forgot about the audience and just had fun. One of my favorite lines was "I ain't your Aunt Eller so don't you call me Aunt Eller you little wort I'm mad at you!" I loved being Aunt Eller and I would give anything to do it again. On all the performances everyone did great. I'm very sad it's all over. I'm glad I had a chance to work with both classes. I really enjoyed the play. I'm very sad it's all over. I'm going to miss the play, and I'll never ever forget it.

Oklahoma!

To tell you the truth, when I first found out what part I had I almost died. Ado Annie was not my first choice.

After a while I got use to the kids teasing me and started to really enjoy being the funny and flirty Ado Annie that I was going to become.

I think this play was the best thing that ever could have happened to me.

After the last performance, Friday night when I got home, I remembered all the time and effort everyone put in to this play and we would never perform it again, tears came to my eyes.

There is one more *very* special memory that I would like to share with you. When one works so closely with a group of children over a long period of time, a special bond seems to form among everyone. It is one of trust, friendship and love, and *nothing* can take its place. This happened with the cast of every show I ever produced but especially, for some reason, with the children of *The King and I*. When that school year ended, and they moved on to sixth grade, I was very sorry to see them go, though I knew we'd see each other and speak as we passed in the hallways the next year. It just wouldn't be the same.

The next year, I was busy with my class and with the planning of our next show. The time was the last day before winter vacation, about ten minutes before school was dismissed for the day. As might be expected, the children were very excited about the coming holiday, and the class was close to bedlam. Suddenly I looked toward the classroom door and saw a large group of children standing quietly, waiting for my attention. It was the entire cast from *The King and I*. How they managed to persuade their sixth-grade teachers to let them leave class I'll never know, but there they were.

I invited them in, and the girl who was standing at the front of the group held out a gift for me—one of the most special gifts I ever expect to receive. It was a small Christmas tree decorated with a picture of every one of those children! Each was attached to an ornament hook, and was hung on the tree—a priceless treasure, which carried with it an unwritten but very clear message that said they would never forget.

Those children are grown now. A few are even married. I think they would be surprised if they ever dropped by my house at Christmastime and saw the tree they gave me sitting in a place of honor in my home. It's there every year, with all those wonderful pictures of some very special people. I'll never forget, either.

14

On Tour

In past years, as our fame spread, we would receive calls from other schools asking if we could do our show for their students. Before we had our own music room/stage, we used to accept one or two of these invitations for each show. We became so well known for the quality of our shows that schools would book us a year in advance. Once we had our own larger facility, we no longer "traveled." There were several reasons for this. (1) We could accommodate larger crowds at our own school, and we therefore suggested that other schools either bring their students to our performance for our own student body or encourage families of their interested students to attend one of our evening community performances. (2) We had more parents who worked full time and their volunteer hours were limited; we needed them to help with makeup, costumes, and other important jobs rather than to transport scenery and props to other schools. (3) Our shows became more and more complicated as our experience grew, and we simply had too many things we would have had to transport.

For those of you who are interested in taking your magnificent show "on the road," however, we offer these suggestions.

Advance Party

If you decide to perform at another school, always send an advance party of adults to the school a few days beforehand. The advance party will check the stage arrangement, piano, microphones, electrical plugs and all technical details. Each school has different facilities, and your team must check out each situation carefully.

Our scenery designer was the authority on the "how to" of transporting scenery and setting it up in a new location. The first question was, if we were using a backdrop, how would we hang it on the new stage? The backdrop gave our show pizzazz, so we wanted to take it with us if possible. If the new stage had a back curtain or bulletin board–type wall, we attached the backdrop with pins or staples. One school had only a cinder block wall behind their stage so they installed furring strips—just for us! Sadly, once we had to leave our backdrop behind because there was no way to install it in the other school.

It is cumbersome to haul flats from building to building. If you are using flats, try to keep their number to an absolute minimum. We never took more than one or two with us.

The next thing to check on was the placement of the piano. It had to be located so that it did not obstruct the view of the audience, but at the same time the cast on stage must be able to make eye contact with the musical accompanist. It was necessary to check for a nearby electrical outlet so that the accompanist could plug in her light. If the piano did not have a light already, she brought her own, plus an extension cord.

Our advance party had to find places where children could change costumes. Many schools had no dressing room facilities in their stage area. School officials who had portable stages located in their cafeteria usually permitted us to create a screen using cafeteria tables, placed folded and upright on either side of the stage. The children changed costumes behind those tables.

The advance party also had to determine where the children would sit while waiting to go on stage. Chairs were necessary for the leads, to preserve their costumes from getting unduly wrinkled or dusty from a less-than-clean floor.

Discipline was never a problem with our young actors. I wish I could say the same for all of our past audiences. Some young children who are not accustomed to having shows or assemblies in their school have not been taught audience manners. They do not know how to behave courteously. We have seen distracted youngsters talk and laugh among themselves during the show. Once we even witnessed a kicking fight in the front row. Our cast members learned to ignore such things and to continue their performance no matter what happened. I remember one cast member who, upon witnessing poor audience behavior, was heard to exclaim, "This is a very immature audience." The adult, while in total agreement with him, could hardly keep from laughing at such wise words from a nine-year-old boy. Our children learn not only how to be good performers; they also learn how to be a good audience. I am happy to say that at most schools where we have performed, the audience has been extremely well behaved.

The advance party would report all the information they gathered on the facilities to me. I then explained to the children the stage arrangement and any unusual situation they would encounter. Then the transportation committee would go to work. It was their job to haul all the scenery, props, lights and extra costumes to the new location. Parents with station wagons, vans or trucks were lined up ahead of time. The adults transported and set up all of our equipment at the school on the afternoon before the children were to perform. Everything was checked and double-checked. All props and costumes were placed exactly where the children were accustomed to looking for them.

Kids on the Road

If our performance was scheduled for 9:30 A.M., the children in costume and makeup were transported in buses furnished by the host school. If there was no bus, we used parent car pools. The children arrived at the host school by 9:15 A.M. The children had a few minutes to look over the stage and locate their props and other costumes. Then they sat in their places backstage and awaited their audience. The students of the host school filed into the auditorium and took their seats. In order to set the proper mood for the play, our cast members sat quietly until the audience was in place. Then our student-announcer rose, went to center stage and introduced the play.

Any unforeseen problems that occurred on stage during the performance would have to be handled by the children in the best way they could. I remember *The Sound of Music*, which ended with the Von Trapp family walking out into the audience as they sang, symbolizing their journey over the mountains to freedom. As the time for this approached, our Maria realized that the audience was seated on the floor, elbow-to-elbow, and there was no aisle for her to walk down as she led her "family" on their journey. When the time came, she took a deep breath and waded into that sea of children, wending her way through them as best she could. As the audience saw what she was doing, they began to make a path for her. Our leading lady saw a problem and she solved it without any adult advice at all!

One year we took our show to a school where one of our secondary leads had been a student the year before. He was very nervous about performing for his former classmates. Because of this, he said one of his lines too early in a scene. If the other actors had continued from the line he said, some of the story would have been lost. They realized this immediately and ad-libbed until they inserted the correct information into the story. It was truly amazing!

Cast members always proved their versatility during performances for these other schools. The way they walked into a strange place and performed like professionals, improvising where necessary, proved just how much they had learned during the months of rehearsals and performances.

Community Encores

One year at least a month after the show ended, we received a call from a senior citizens' home asking that we bring the show to them. We decided to accept the invitation. We had to go back into rehearsal because the children had not practiced in a month. Not a single child had any objection to doing this! The adults were astounded at how quickly the children were able to bring the play to perfection. In just a few rehearsals, they were ready to perform again. Those senior citizens loved them. It was a heartwarming performance and worth the effort!

Another year we were approached by someone from a nationwide cable network. Would we be interested in performing a short segment of that year's show for their educational program, *Inside Your Schools*? We responded in the affirmative, and that short segment was not only shown once, but appeared over and over again during the next year.

We received a call from a local television station asking us to appear on one of their programs aimed directly at children. We jumped at the chance, and performed a 20-minute segment of that year's show. This was also rebroadcast over and over again on that station.

The International Children's Festival

Another year a notice appeared in a major Washington, D.C., newspaper announcing May auditions for the International Children's

Festival to be held at Wolf Trap Farm Park. The Festival would be a three-day nonstop collection of acts for the education and entertainment of children. Wolf Trap is the only national park for the performing arts and is located near our town. Auditions were scheduled for Memorial Day weekend and the Festival for Labor Day weekend. The adults having the principal responsibilities for the show discussed the intriguing possibility of auditioning for the Festival. If we decided to audition and were fortunate enough to be accepted, it would mean summer rehearsals. We decided to contact the parents and children to learn who might be interested in participating and which families would be in town over those two holiday weekends. We also decided to expand our group to include not only the current cast of *Annie Get Your Gun* but also a group from the previous year's play, *The Music Man*. The child who played the lead in that show was supremely talented, and we felt he and his classmates deserved a chance to participate too.

We held a joint meeting of the two casts to tell them of our idea and to determine their reaction. As we expected, they were thrilled, but would their parents agree? We sent a letter home asking who would be in town for auditions, late August rehearsals and Labor Day performances. Just think of the excitement in those homes that evening! Our answer came the next day when the children returned to school. Every single child from *Annie Get Your Gun* would be able to participate and 25 children from *The Music Man* also replied in the affirmative—60 children in all! Some of them had persuaded their parents to revise vacation plans so they would be available when needed. Nothing more clearly demonstrates the dedication of the children—and their parents—to our shows.

Before Audition Day arrived, the director of the Festival said that she would like to see the 15-minute segment we had planned for *The Music Man* and a 30-minute excerpt of *Annie Get Your Gun*. This would enable her to see enough to determine the quality of the children's work. A quick rewrite on both scripts produced 15 minutes of dynamic songs from *The Music Man* and 30 minutes of music and dialogue from *Annie Get Your Gun*, highlighting the best parts and including our "smash" finale. We spent two weeks in rehearsals so that the segments we had chosen would flow smoothly. Though the cast of *The Music Man* had not rehearsed in 14 months, you would never have known it to watch them. Even the first rehearsal was superb!

Memorial weekend and Audition Day arrived. Because the

Our Annie Oakley sings "There's No Business Like Show Business" at the International Children's Festival.

school was closed for the weekend, we designated two homes as makeup stations for the two casts. Each home had more eager makeup volunteers and car pool drivers than we could possibly use. The children reported in costume and were soon into makeup and on their way.

We arrived at the audition site 45 minutes before our appointed time only to find that auditions were running one hour behind schedule. How were we to keep 60 costumed children clean and well-behaved for that length of time? We decided to take them into the auditorium so that they could watch the other groups audition. They filed in and took their seats without so much as a whisper. Some of the fathers in the group, used to seeing their rambunctious offspring bouncing around home, could not believe their eyes!

I reported to the director of the Festival when we arrived. She was in charge of auditions; in fact, she was the sole judge and jury. There were lots of acts; it took four full days for all of them to audition. She told me that since auditions were running behind schedule, we would be allowed only 30 minutes for our two groups instead of the 45 minutes we had rehearsed. I quickly reevaluated our script and decided to eliminate one full scene and the dance number from *Annie Get Your Gun*, giving each show equal time. I could not talk to the children in the auditorium so I had to wait until they were backstage, ready to perform, before I told them of the necessary "cut." Our young dancers were extremely disappointed.

The cast of *The Music Man* went on stage, and our young dynamo sang with every ounce of talent and energy he had. The Festival director looked at me in amazement and asked, "Where did you find *him*?" After that cast was finished, the other one took its place on stage, hiding disappointment at having its part shortened, and prepared to begin. The director said to them, "If you are as good as the last group, I don't need to see much." They began to perform, doing a better job than they had ever done in any performance to date. I was so proud of them! Then right in the middle of the first scene, the director said, "Thank you. Now I'd like to see the finale." The children simply stopped, reassembled in their finale formation, and proceeded as though they did this sort of thing every day of the week. I could not believe it! Ten-year-old children! The audition lasted seven minutes instead of the planned 30.

As we left the auditorium, we were stunned at the way our audition time had been cut. The parents felt their children's keen disappointment at not being allowed to show what they could really do, but marveled at the way each child handled the situation—like a thoroughly professional performer.

Now the waiting began. The question was asked daily by scores of people—children and adults—"Have you heard from the Festival yet?" Nerves frayed and hopes sagged. Finally on the last day of school for the year, I received the long-awaited phone call. Both casts had been accepted into the Festival! When our school principal made the announcement to the entire student body over the public address system, the cheer that arose from the children almost lifted the roof from the building! It was a moment to savor that I will never forget!

So when the final curtain has fallen, do not dispose of your scenery. Roll it up and store it in someone's basement. You never know when you will need it again. Though you will return all borrowed props, it is easy to keep a list of them and their owners. Who knows when you will need them again for another performance of your show or even a new one another year. Once a parent has had a child in one of your shows, that parent will be most anxious to lend you things for another show. There is a camaraderie among past and present cast families. We all appreciate each other and the work that goes into a show. We never lose that feeling of closeness that develops. We all feel part of a very special group that has accomplished something out of the ordinary. It's a nice feeling!

15

Checklist and Reflections

And so you have it—how to put on a Broadway show with children. We have shared with you our ideas and our hard-won expertise, along with anecdotes that we hope have given you a chuckle or two. Your creativity will take care of anything we may have missed. What follows is a master operating plan, so that no detail is forgotten, and a list of those intangibles gained by the children and you. Give it a chance. We wish you luck. The benefit to the children is incalculable. You will never regret the undertaking.

Countdown Checklist

Summer
(About eight or nine months before your first performance)
➤ Choose and revise the script. Divide the script into sections for rehearsal purposes.
➤ Apply for the license to perform your play.

September
(About seven months before your first performance)
➤ Begin costume and scenery designs.
➤ Make a list of needed props.

October
(Six months before performances)
➤ Hold a meeting with the parents of your children. Discuss all plans for the show. Recruit volunteers for all jobs and committees.

➤ Tell children that those who do not keep up with their school work will not be considered for a major part.

November
(Five months before performances)
➤ Pass out scripts to children. Read the play aloud to them.

➤ Tell the children what sections of the scripts will be used in auditions. Pass out an Audition Script (usually one page long) to each child.

➤ Notify your boys that they will be required to wear stage makeup in dress rehearsals and in all performances.

➤ Try to find a local professional group that is performing the show you are doing. Arrange a trip for all interested children and parents.

➤ Send a letter home, telling parents about auditions, and about costume requirements for the different parts in the play.

➤ Tell girls to consider trying out for boys' parts.

➤ Pass out a Part Preference Form to each child. Ask them to fill it out at home, with parent help. Collect these the next day.

➤ Make out a Master Part Preference Form, summarizing the information you received from the children's forms. Give a copy to each member of the audition committee.

➤ Send home for parent signature: Permission slips for auditions and for rehearsals.

➤ Auditions and casting

December
(Four months before performances)
➤ Announce the cast.

➤ Visit the homes of the major characters to go over their lines with them and parents. This is an optional activity, but I have found it helpful on occasion.

➤ Children memorize all lines during the winter Holiday.

January
(Three months before performances)
➤ Buy any fabric that must be purchased in bulk. This could be done earlier if you have time.

➤ Post a rehearsal schedule in the classroom.

➤ REHEARSALS BEGIN!

➤ Children should study lines *each night* for the next day's rehearsal.

➤ Practice one script section per day, blocking out action, entrances and exits. Proceed through the entire play in this manner. It will take about two weeks. Then start over, and go through the play again.

➤ Tape-record all rehearsals; listen for errors, and point these out to students.

➤ Set entrance cues in the middle of lines instead of at the ends.

➤ Stress the following:

(1) Speak in a loud voice.

(2) Speak slowly; pronounce every syllable.

(3) Use the backstage hand for gesturing.

(4) Look at the person to whom you are speaking, and at the one speaking to you.

(5) Do not mouth the words someone else is saying.

➤ Musical director works on songs before school, sets her own schedule of lessons and gives a schedule to each child.

➤ Begin to choreograph dance routines. This can be done sooner if you have time.

➤ Scenery designer begins gridding and drawing the backdrop and/or other scenery.

➤ A volunteer builds the scenery flat(s).

➤ Costume Committee cuts out fabric for those wearing identical costumes made from the fabric you purchased in bulk.

➤ Assign one member of the Costume Committee to each parent needing help with sewing.

February
(Two months before performances)

➤ Begin to rehearse two or three script parts per day.

➤ Add the songs to rehearsals.

➤ Begin to gather props and use them in rehearsals.

➤ Invite parents to attend rehearsals.

➤ Check with the children to see if anyone is having any costume problems. Pass the information along to the costume coordinator so she can call the parents of those having difficulty to see if she can help.

➤ Paint scenery. This will take approximately two hours.

➤ Begin dance rehearsals if you have not already done so.

➤ Toward the end of the month begin rehearsals on the finale routine. Use regular rehearsal time, since the entire cast will be involved.

➤ Hold a contest for the design of your program cover.

➤ Keep a running list of all adults who help with any phase of play production. You must recognize them by publishing their names in the program insert.

➤ Cast Party Committee meets to discuss and solidify plans regarding food, punch and gifts to volunteers.

➤ Send home a letter, inviting all cast families to the cast party. List your needs for refreshments. Request money to pay for punch, napkins and gifts to volunteers who do not have a child in the show. (We request $10 from each family, plus about three dozen cookies.)

March
(One month before performances)
➤ Move rehearsals to performance stage.

➤ Rehearse one entire act each day during the first half of the month, including all songs and dances.

➤ Add the encore to your finale routine.

➤ Type the program and send it to the printer.

➤ Arrange for cast photographer to take pictures during the first dress rehearsal. Videotaping may be arranged for the night of the last performance if so desired.

➤ Check with the children to see that all costumes are finished.

➤ Contact the chairperson of your Makeup Committee, and suggest that she notify her helpers of the dates and times they will be needed.

➤ Send home a schedule of all dress rehearsals and performances, dates and times children are required to arrive for costuming and/or makeup.

➤ Find out from cast members how many reserved seats each will need for family members at the community performances. Make up seat reservation signs.

➤ During the last week of the month rehearse the entire play daily. Begin rehearsals at 2:00 P.M. and continue until 4:30 P.M. if necessary.

➤ During the last week of the month have the student stage crew work with the actual backdrop and/or flat(s).

➤ Double-check the makeup, to make sure you have everything you need.

➤ Friday—First dress rehearsal. Cast photographer takes pictures.
1:00 P.M.—Cast dresses in costumes.

1:15 P.M.—Makeup is applied to cast faces.

2:00 P.M.—Dress rehearsal.

April—First Week

➤ Monday—Second dress rehearsal.

1:00 P.M.—Cast dresses in costumes.

1:15 P.M.—Makeup is applied to cast faces.

2:00 P.M.—Dress rehearsal.

➤ Tuesday—Student Performance.

8:00 P.M.—Cast arrives for costuming and makeup.

9:15 P.M.—Performance for students.

➤ Cast members take costumes home.

➤ Wednesday—NO REHEARSAL

➤ Thursday—Community Performance.

6:30 P.M.—Cast arrives *in costume* for makeup.

7:30 P.M.—First community performance.

➤ Friday—Community Performance.

6:30 P.M.—Cast arrives *in costume* for makeup.

7:30 P.M.—Community Performance. Gifts given to volunteers at the end of the performance.

➤ 9:00 P.M.—Cast party in the cafeteria for all cast members, their families, and out-of-town relatives or friends.

➤ 10:30 P.M.—Director gives a party at her home for those adults who helped her most on the play. This is an optional activity, but we really enjoy reliving a glorious night!

If you are using a stage outside of your home school, as we did for many years, your first and second weeks of April might look something like this.

April—First Week

➤ Monday—Rehearse on junior high school stage. Remember that the first day will probably be chaotic!

➤ Tuesday—Rehearse on junior high school stage.

➤ Wednesday—Rehearse on junior high school stage.

➤ Thursday—NO REHEARSAL. (When we performed on the junior high school stage, we gave only one evening community performance—Friday evening.

➤ Friday—Community Performance.

6:30 P.M.—Children arrive in costume, ready for makeup

7:30 P.M.—Community Performance.

9:15 P.M.—Cast Party in cafeteria of your home school.
10:30—Small party at the home of the director.

Third or Fourth Week: Optional

Take your show to other schools. Send out an advance party of adults to the host school. Have them check the following:

➤ (1) Is there any way to install the backdrop?

➤ (2) Where will the children change costumes?

➤ (3) Where will cast members sit when not on stage?

➤ (4) Where will the piano be placed so that the children can see the accompanist yet so that the piano will not block the view of the audience?

Arrive at the host school fifteen minutes before the scheduled performance so cast members can look over the facilities for themselves.

What Have the Children Gained?

The play is now over. It is time to sit back and think about your activities of the last few months. What are the benefits that the children have gained from this experience?

(1) They have developed a great deal of self-confidence. Even the shyest child feels that he has accomplished something he never thought possible.

(2) They have learned to work in a group. Each child must do his very best in order for the entire show to be successful.

(3) The children and their parents have worked jointly on a project, and have come closer together in the process.

(4) The children have learned to organize their time so that they are able to handle homework, play rehearsals plus all the other activities in which they choose to participate.

(5) They have had an opportunity to take part in an activity they will remember for the rest of their lives.

(6) They will become drama critics with no small skill. They know what goes into making a good play, and they are able to better judge the quality of any performance they may attend in the future.

What Have You Gained?

You have given much; what have you gained?

(1) You have learned to budget your time to a greater degree than before. You are able to balance grading papers with rehearsals and many other tasks connected with the play and still have time for a home life.

(2) You have given these children an opportunity to participate in a single activity that will influence their future lives in many aspects.

(3) Your ability to assess children, their strengths and weaknesses, has been remarkably sharpened, making you a better teacher.

(4) You have been given a most valuable gift—that of friendship. Those parents who have worked so long and hard with you over so many months have become much more than just parents of your students. They have become very good friends. Some of them will be back to work with you next year.

(5) You have learned many skills that make a good director. You have gained experience and ideas for use with future shows.

(6) You have watched your students grow and mature in a way not often experienced by adults outside the family, even teachers.

(7) You have added a new interest, one that will reach into many corners of your life. From now on you will always be hunting new scripts, new ways of doing things. You have found a new hobby, as it begins to occupy your less-busy moments.

(8) You have experienced true joy at something that you have done well. What a gratifying feeling that is!

(9) For what it's worth, you will be remembered by these children as the teacher who "made it all possible."

Index

Numbers in **boldface** *refer to pages with photographs.*